with the
compliments of

Nova Scotia Museum Complex

Nova Scotia

**Department of
Education**

D0905566

HOUSES OF
NOVA SCOTIA

Allen Penney

HOUSES OF NOVA SCOTIA

An illustrated guide to Architectural Style Recognition

by
Allen Penney

co-published by
Formac Publishing Company and
The Nova Scotia Museum
Halifax, Nova Scotia
1989

Canadian Cataloguing in Publication Data
Penney, Allen.
    Houses of Nova Scotia
    ISBN 0-88780-072-6
1. Architecture, Domestic — Nova Scotia —
Guide-books.   I.   Nova Scotia Museum.
II. Title.
NA7242.N6P46 1989   728'.09716   C89-098569-3

Co-published by Formac Publishing and the Nova Scotia Museum as part
of the Education Resource Services Program of the Department of Education, Province of Nova Scotia.

Minister: The Hon. Ronald C. Giffin, Q.C.
Deputy Minister: Blenis J. Nicholson

A Product of the Nova Scotia Government Co-publishing Program.

Printed in Nova Scotia, Canada

Formac Publishing Company Limited
5502 Atlantic Street
Halifax, Nova Scotia
B3H 1G4

5 4 3 2 1   89 90 91 92 93 94

To RAAP and EFP
for planting the interest,
to JCP, SP and CP for extreme patience,
to ME and ER for encouragement.

Contents

Preface

This book was written to provide some answers for those people who get asked "How old is it?" or "What style is that house?" They may be parents, teachers, students or guides for summer visitors. They may be asked in the car, in the garden or on a walk. It is hoped that the size of the book makes it portable yet comprehensive, that the information is accessible and the descriptions clear. There is an underlying hope that its use will bring enjoyment through a deeper understanding of our heritage.

Some years ago now, the author conceived an idea for a book that would do for houses what has long been done for birds—a field guide. Each page would have a general profile of each style plus information on easily recognized features and even some identification marks of a subtle shift within a group. There would also be a crude dating system. It might then be possible for anyone to claim a "sighting." Although a number of American books on style recognition have been written recently, none satisfactorily covers the architecture used in Nova Scotia.

Under the author's supervision, two preliminary studies of domestic architecture in Nova Scotia were made by Teresa Janik while she was a student at the Technical University of Nova Scotia. The author then enlarged and reworked the information from these preliminary studies in preparation for a 1979 workshop sponsored by the Federation of Museums, Heritage and Historical Societies of Nova Scotia (now the Federation of Nova Scotian Heritage). There was sufficient positive response to this first workshop that Elizabeth Ross, Executive Director of the Federation, organized a second for the following year.

During 1982 the author received a grant from the President's Fund at the Technical University of Nova Scotia, which distributes money from the Social Sciences and Humanities Research Council of Canada. This allowed Teresa Janik to gather still more information, and so the proposed book grew in both scope and depth. The final result is before you.

Among those who have helped make this book a reality are Professor Anthony Jackson, who has been both a supportive and patient friend, and Professor Kent Hurley, who edited it at an early stage.

Others to whom the author is indebted in various ways are Marie Elwood and Scott Robson of the Nova Scotia Museum; Christina Cameron, who worked at the time with the Canadian Inventory of Historic Buildings, Ottawa; Garry Shutlak and Margaret Campbell of the Public Archives of Nova Scotia; and Alan Cash, late of the Heritage Unit of the Department of Culture, Recreation and Fitness of the Province of Nova Scotia. Both Professor Barry Moody of Acadia University and Ann Hale of Parks Canada, Halifax, gave valuable help in special areas. Many others who helped must go unnamed.

John Hennigar-Shuh, Curator of Publications at the Nova Scotia Museum, Kathy Kaulbach, formerly of the Museum, and the Publications Committee of the Museum must also be thanked for publishing this book.

The author is especially grateful to Essy Baniassad, Dean of the Faculty of Architecture, Technical University of Nova Scotia, typists Donna Morrison and Jeanne Melanson, and student Lim Thien Pink of the Faculty of Architecture at the Technical University of Nova Scotia for their encouragement and help.

Elizabeth Eve deserves recognition as the editor of the final version, where the author learned clarity of style. The author was taught by her father at the Architectural Association School of Architecture, London, England.

To all these the author is deeply grateful. Any errors are his and his alone.

Allen Penney, Halifax, Nova Scotia, 1988

Introduction

The aim of this book is to explain and clarify the architecture of Nova Scotia houses in simple language and pictures. It is designed to be used as a field guide so that the reader might be able to identify the style of a dwelling, its approximate date and the source of the style.

As a basis for the book, about 5,000 houses have been studied, or two percent of the houses in the province. The proportion of early houses studied is significantly greater than that of more recent ones. This sample was dependent on the collections of photographs accessible to the general public and on some private photograph collections, notably the author's. It seems reasonable to point out that 70 percent of the houses in Nova Scotia are single-family detached houses, and that many of these are of recent construction. This means that there is a bias in this book towards older houses. Indeed, some of the house styles included here will not be easy to find and, in some cases, the examples used are truly unique. Fewer than 1,000 houses in this sample had been given dates, and many of these dates proved to be unreliable. Dates quoted are believed to be accurate for the individual houses, whereas the dates given for the span of each style are based on examples as well as personal judgement. Until there is a larger body of well-researched data, some dating may turn out to be uncertain.

Public holdings of photographs rarely contain dated material. In fact, the photograph collections tend to be patchy in their scope; often having been formed by individuals as a hobby and thus having limited time or geographic ranges. Photographs are rarely documented and so may be quite unreliable since the main source of the information was probably oral, usually provided by the owner. It is unfortunate that home owners, flattered by the attention given their houses by transient photographers, have sometimes been led to exaggerate the age of the buildings.

Age must be quoted with caution. Precise dates of initial construction are rare, and of subsequent alteration, even rarer. A complex title search of the property may not reveal any more facts than dates, which establish a period when the house may have been built. When a date can be found, you ask is it for this house or for an earlier one? A title search may not disclose whether a building has been replaced, altered or even moved from another location.

For example, in 1833 Thomas Chandler Haliburton bought some land in Windsor, and in 1835 advertised a house on another site for rent. It may be assumed that between these dates the new house was constructed, but it is not proven. During its lifetime, his house has undergone many changes. At present, the paint is six years old, the roof is nine, the main visible roof structure fifty-four and the belvedere seventy-five. The fire-blackened earlier belvedere is still partly recognizable, however, and is over one hundred years old. Each alteration is in a different style and made of materials true to the age of alteration. Therefore how old is this house? And what is its style?

To accurately describe the house, we would find it difficult to find any word more appropriate than "altered." Unravelling the sequence of the alterations is not only fascinating in itself but also supplements the appreciation of the house as it stands today.

Considerable time and effort have been expended to establish a data base for this book with adequate geographical distribution. Style and age ranges have been estimated more by available date than by exact proportional representation. The sample appears to be large enough to avoid false conclusions.

Another bias in the data is notable, though possibly forgivable: the houses used are all visible, rather than secluded. Apart from the difficulty in getting illustrations of secluded private property, the very idea of the book is to cover those houses that can be seen. The significance of this bias may be small enough not to sway the result too much, but the responsibility to honour privacy seems to be appropriate to the Nova Scotia lifestyle.

In selecting illustrations the author has tried to use only those houses that are still standing. This does not mean that those houses that are shown will still be standing when a visit is made, but it is intended that most buildings illustrated are still extant so as to make the hunt worthwhile. Some houses that are known to have been destroyed are included as the best available illustrations of a style.

The economy of Nova Scotia has had a marked effect on the architectural development in the region. During the first 100 years of British rule there was a continuous succession of wars and threats of war. Money was scarce, the economy was dependent on military funds, and people lived in an atmosphere of permanent insecurity, at least to the point where there was little incentive to invest in grand new houses. Later, during the mid-to late-Victorian period, there was a buoyant trade with Europe as well as with the United States, and the housing stock of this period reflects the economic boom.

In both town and country the large stock of older dwellings can be attributed to the reluctance to destroy the old but still serviceable houses when times were hard. It may also be partly due to the large number of inhabitants who, even if rich enough to develop their property, prefer to hold on to their old houses.

As the richest province at the time of Confederation and one of the poorer ones now, Nova Scotia has felt relatively little pressure from developers to cause wholesale destruction of portions of the housing stock. Probably the greatest losses of significant older houses have been from numerous fires that destroyed large parts of Nova Scotia towns. This has resulted in a relatively small sample in central and urban areas. Nevertheless a substantial collection of houses built of wood remains for study. A good representation from each period of development is extant, and they are sometimes concentrated in areas small enough to be covered on foot. Truro, Lunenburg and the south end of Halifax, for example, can provide three good afternoons of walking, standing and looking.

How is it possible to balance "progress" with "heritage"? The population of Nova Scotia has recently exceeded the level at Con-federation, and the pace of development has been picking up. Significant changes are taking place in towns and in the countryside. Houses and even whole streets are being destroyed for new forms of development, while in other cases the develop-ment incorporates old buildings, even houses, in new forms of building. It might be conjectured that far more damage has taken place in the last few years than in all previous history. The introduction of new siding materials and the panic countermeasures of governments to the energy crisis of the 1970s have caused untold damage to the housing stock and irretrievably destroyed the appearance of large numbers of older, elegant dwellings. In addition, a less visible and more pernicious result of these "instant" renovations is the structural rot beginning to emerge from the improper installation of insulation materials. Through the CHIP programme, $100,000,000 was injected into the province's economy in the interests of energy conservation. Some of the injurious effects to the houses are not irreversible, but it is unlikely that a reversal will take place—the siding removed and the trim replaced.

It is difficult to balance conservation of houses with conservation of energy, but they are not necessarily antagonistic. There just happened to be a rapid escalation in the cost of heating fuels and no indication that prices would ever come down.

Paradoxically, the heritage conservation movement has also contributed to the destruction of much that was architecturally fine. By allowing legislation to deal almost exclusively with the exteriors of old buildings, preservationists have contributed to an architectural environment with no more integrity than the facadism of a film set. Too often the preservationists have seen the problem as black and white—either keep or destroy. However, in many parts of the world developers are required to harmonize, in scale, without the constraint of an imposed style. Examples of disharmony can be seen in older houses that have been split up into multiple dwelling units and extended. The addition of a group of dwelling units to an old house alters the scale of the whole, diminishing the original house. Gone is the house and gone, too, is the scale for all the surrounding houses.

Present legislation is timid and fails to satisfy the conservers and the developers. Where legislation could most easily be improved is in requiring an archival set of measured drawings and photographs to show what has to be removed to allow the development. The cost of such records is negligible in the context of development costs and profits.

As with energy, old buildings are not a renewable resource, despite many architectural attempts to fool the casual observer. This book is intended to assist in discriminating the real from the replica and, by assisting in the better understanding of our past, to make the present and future more enjoyable.

Many homeowners will be tempted to seek out "their" house in this book and will no doubt be frustrated when they cannot find it. Except in a few cases, space limitations have meant that the illustrations tend towards the typical and the broad descriptions, rather than the specific ones.

Ultimately there is only one purpose in writing this book; it is to promote understanding and enjoyment of the architectural splendour of Nova Scotia—a splendour not of fine palaces but of common houses.

How to use this book

Houses of Nova Scotia is designed as a practical guide: not only is it portable, it is assembled to make the information easily accessible.

As this book deals with the exteriors of houses, and not their interiors, it sets out to help you identify and date houses and learn to recognize elements of their style.

The first part of the book is about the general picture—style, form, ways of separating information about a building. To make accurate observations and responses to architectural style as seen in Nova Scotia, one must know how to look. The description of parts helps the reader know what to look for. Every building is unique, so a true field guide to houses is not possible, but armed with this book one can piece together the history and origins of a house.

The next section, Architectural Style, is the introduction to this method of observation. *Use the Glossary to broaden the picture with new terms and precise information, and then the Guide to Styles will become a useful tool to unlock the key to the houses in your town, city or village.*

The Guide to Styles is in chronological sequence and follows the same format throughout the book. On the left-hand pages are the introductions to each architectural style, which are intended to describe the origins, context and the main distinguishing features of each style. On the right-hand pages are the visual aids to style recognition and at the top of these pages are isometric drawings of the forms of the houses. Beneath this is an elevation, followed by a door, window, and sometimes construction and a significant detail. In combination these elements comprise the total description of the style.

Because the same format is used for most styles, it is possible to flip the pages to find the best approximation. Beware the superficial likenesses: much copying took place as style succeeded style and as additions were made in a different style from the original house. Because of the inevitable small number of examples, it may not be possible to find an exact likeness.

The names of the styles are not standardized but all have been carefully chosen to assist in understanding the house.

Note: letters in parentheses after the locations refer to: (A) altered, (D) destroyed or (R) reconstructed. Where no location is given, the illustration is of a general principle.

Architectural Style

Architectural Style: a definite type of architecture,
distinguished by special characteristics of structure or
ornamentation.

Oxford English Dictionary

Style in all its manifestations, from hairstyles to microwave ovens,
from cars to pets, is a reflection of social and economic change. In
houses, style is expressed in the form, the overall shape of the
building, the significant elements such as doors, windows and
roof and, especially in the context of Nova Scotia, in ornamentation.

It is possible in architecture to find more than one style used
at a time, even combined, in the same structure. This guide will
assist in isolating and identifying styles. By checking dates, it may
be possible to detect whether the building was built initially using
several styles or whether it was altered over time, with each
successive alteration being in the style of its day.

Style is a current that runs through the fabric of society; it
appears to be controlled by a similar cycle of events as any other
aspect of man's endeavour. The original burst of energy is followed by development, refinement and acceptance. At its
maturity it reflects a popular statement of its times. There is a peak
followed by a rapid decline and, eventually, rejection. In this book,
architectural style is examined in the houses of one specific
geographic region during one short period of history—1605-1988,
and while the story of style in Nova Scotia is quite ordinary in that
it fits the general picture of western society for this period, the
province is special in that it has a broad collection of architectural
styles within a relatively small geographic area.

The difficulty in assessing whether a group of buildings
justifies its own style has been approached rather loosely. Using
the Oxford English Dictionary definition, a "type" of building
might be isolated, hence the Halifax and Lunenburg houses,

which share a common form, and Log houses, which share a common material. Within the type there exist style variations performing a minor role. Obviously the reader must take care to not read too much into what might be an arbitrary categorization. In general, style books can be misleading because individual authors select different criteria as the basis of their style definition.

The reasons for the emergence of a new style may vary. At one time it is the revival of an historic form, for example, the Classical Revival; at another, it is the result of a manufacturing improvement, such as the large sheets of glass used in modern styles.

Nowadays it is not uncommon to see five or six contemporary styles in juxtaposition on one street, but during the eighteenth century style was relatively consistent within a particular culture. The use of English, Dutch and Spanish designs was evident throughout each of the colonial empires. It was during the nineteenth century that styles began to change with increasing frequency and to cross cultural borders.

The great architectural historian, Sir Nikolaus Pevsner, summed up the architectural history of the nineteenth century in just one word: "historicism." In Nova Scotia, the general history of architectural style after 1750 conforms to this definition, that is, a succession of revivals of historic styles. Some styles have been revived so many times that it may now be difficult to find any visual connection to the original example. In whole or in part, we can find references to styles from as wide a range of sources as Ancient Egyptian, Greek, Roman, English and Italian Gothic, Italian and French Renaisssance. Examples in Nova Scotia are usually made of wood, whereas all the originals were made of masonry.

The history of style in the twentieth century seems to be a continuation of the nineteenth century 'historicism' despite the early burst of energy in the creation of a brand new style—the Modern Movement, more recently known as the International style.

In contrast to the eighteenth century, where one style lasted a century, nowadays once a style has reached maturity it seems to be very short lived. It would appear that the main development of a style is the period of its popularity, and that the peak of popularity lasts only for a moment before it withers away. Concurrent styles, such as the Gothic Revival, Italianate and Second Empire styles of the Victorian period, advanced at different speeds and reached substantially different levels of maturity before their demise.

"New" styles are introduced in a variety of ways: through an individual immigrant or group replicating the buildings of their homeland; through books of designs, for example, Palladio's designs from Italy republished in England and brought to North America; through itinerant workmen carrying with them the habits and forms from their own apprenticeships; through technological development in materials and machinery; and through large organizations—the colonial government, the federal government and railway companies, all of whom export design from their central seats of power.

For the early immigrants there was often no alternative way to build than to use methods from their country of origin. Time was a serious issue with an impending severe winter. In the mid-eighteenth century, settlers from New England arrived with prefabricated houses. Later on, available materials were put to use with some very interesting results, as with the sod houses of the Prairies. Once the population had become established in the nineteenth century, then new immigrants were able to rent existing houses or had help to build in the current style.

In addition to books of designs, the contemporary "literary" influence on style is magazines. Once an idea becomes fashionable it is groomed by the popular magazines into a marketable product, and this is as true today for house design as it is for shoes. In no time at all a new style is accepted from coast to coast.

The influence of technology was never more evident than during the industrial revolution, especially during the middle of the nineteenth century. Power tools, which made mass production of decorative elements easy and cheap, brought about an explosion of enthusiasm for the machine-made mouldings, brackets and fretwork. The surface texture of the buildings changed from largely plain to heavily modelled and encrusted. The ultimate use of the prefabricated detail came with the spindle and lathework seen conspicuously at the eaves and porches of the late nineteenth century houses. The machined parts were held in stock or made to order from stock cutter blades and, therefore, could be combined in different ways. If parts from different styles were combined, then a new style was generated. The number of styles increased, and the duration of their use diminished as time passed.

New styles may stem from a copy of an older existing building or may begin as a reaction to current building habits. The Neo-classical borrowed from antiquity; the Modern Movement reacted against late-nineteenth century pluralism and extravagance.

Transition from one style to another can be rapid or very slow indeed. There may be a sudden break of style or there may be an absorption of the old by the new. Some absorbed details may be used again in a later style; details such as the Gothic Revival hood moulding over a window reappear several style changes later.

Acceptance of a new style may be slow but, once embraced, may take a very long time to be discarded; again, Gothic Revival, which was popular for about fifty years, spread its influence over about one hundred years. Of course the style was modified endlessly.

Style seems to be relatively immune from the effects of world history. The wars of Napoleon did not prevent English women from wearing French city-style clothing or French men from wearing English country-style clothes. Despite the ravages of the Second World War, German designs were eagerly reviewed and copied by British architects in post-war Britain. On the other hand, the energy crisis of the 1970s has had some negative effect through siding subsidies, and has also generated its own style, which I have termed Ecology.

Decline of a style can often be seen in the details that become coarse and exaggerated over time. The transfer of a style from one region to another can mean the erosion of a regional characteristic that initially established the style. There is usually a decline in the popularity of a style before another takes over, but there may be several new styles still in their infancy before one grows to maturity over its siblings.

Each style represented in Nova Scotia has a similar life-cycle—

birth is followed by development, maturity and then decline, after which the style may be absorbed or extinguished by the next style.

The average homeowner's awareness of the issues of style selection may have changed very little over the years, but the options have increased dramatically. While the plan remains the same, the appearance may vary from France to England, from eighteenth to twentieth century, and from log to stone. The large number of styles available suggests that what we now have is not so much style as styling.

As many houses combine styles, it has never been the intention that this book should provide a quick source of reference for a style "title" or handle. Since houses in Nova Scotia are commonly built of wood, style is more apparent in ornamentation on the exterior than through hidden structural systems. Although some mention of the structure is included in this book, most of the style description is derived from ornamentation.

Whatever else this book is used for, its purpose is to help inform the general public about one very tangible reminder of Nova Scotia history, its houses. In 1910, Beckles Willson called this "the Province that has been passed by." This may have been so. Certainly, for those who like looking at architecture, one of the advantages of the lack of radical development in Nova Scotia has been that it has allowed the accumulation of a remarkable stock of houses for our study and enjoyment. One outstanding example of the richness of our architectural heritage is that the entire story of the development of the Lunenburg dormer window—the distinguishing mark of its community—can still be seen intact in Lunenburg today.

By isolating style we must not fall into the trap of believing that style is supremely important of itself. Style is merely a convenient visual way of examining the changes in the history of groups of people and what they leave behind them.

Glossary

This glossary contains references to descriptions and illustrations included in this book. It endeavours to explain the parts of a house and to supply enough information to satisfy the needs of general readers. It is not a substitute for any number of other sources and reference books—dictionaries, encyclopedias and glossaries of architectural terms, etc.

The Bibliography on page 143 lists some reference books that will give detailed definitions and a comprehensive index of architectural terms.

Arcade A series of arches

Arch In masonry, a spanning method using wedge-shaped blocks, permitting a longer span than a lintel would provide

Architrave a. Lowermost part of an entablature
b. A door or window moulding

Ashlar Smooth stone finish

Artificial stone veneer A thin covering to give the appearance of a solid wall

Balustrade Row of posts (balusters) and a rail at the edge of stairs or roof

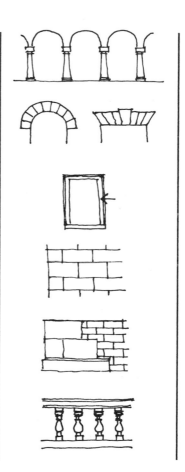

Bargeboard Board at the end of a gable, sometimes ornately carved

Bartizan An overhanging corner turret on a wall

Batten Narrow strips of wood, also see "Board and Batten"

Batter Inward lean to a wall or column face

Bay a. Bay window
b. A section of a building repeated several times

Beam Heavy frame member, usually supporting other loads

Bellcast Curved shape resulting in a lower pitch at the bottom of a roof slope

Belvedere Small roof-top enclosure especially made for a view

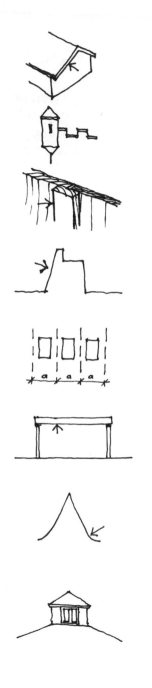

Board and Batten Exterior cladding of alternate wide and narrow strips of wood nailed vertically to the exterior wall

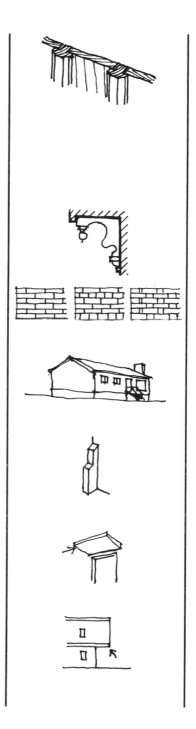

Boss Ornament such as at the intersection in a vaulted roof

Bracket Support under a wide overhang

Brickwork Clay bricks assembled with mortar

Bungalow Small single-storied dwelling

Buttress A mass of masonry or brickwork projecting from or built against a wall for support

Canopy Ornamental roof-like structure, especially over a door

Cantilever A projecting beam or portion of a building without additional support

Capital The top of a column, often decorated

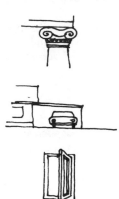

Carport Covered area for a car, usually attached to a house

Casement A window with the sash hinged on the side

Cladding General term including all types of material used to protect a building from the weather, usually walls

Clapboard Strips of wood nailed on the exterior of walls to overlap and shed water. Early ones are hand-shaped, later ones are sawn

Clerestory window Upper level window for light, not view

Colonnade Row of columns carrying a continuous beam or arches

Column An upright support, usually circular in plan, comprising a base, shaft and capital

Composite One of the styles of Orders

Corbel Short cantilever, usually masonry

Corinthian One of the styles of Orders

Cornice The projecting finish at the top of a wall or entablature

Crenellation Imitation battlements, decorative indentations at the top of a wall

Cresting Ornamental finish along the ridge of a roof

Cupola Small domed structure either on its own or on the roof

Dentils Tooth-like projections in a cornice

Doric One of the styles of Orders

Dormer window Window set in a
gable projecting from a sloping roof

Double-hung Refers to a vertical
sliding sash window; originally the
sashes were counterbalanced with
lead weights

Dressed stone Stone finished to a
smooth or moulded surface

Eaves The underside of a roof
projection

Elevation The face of a building or the
vertical projection of that face as a
scale drawing

End grain Grain at cross section of tree
or lumber

Engaged column Column partly
absorbed into the wall so that it is
not free-standing

Entablature The topmost group of
mouldings in an Order

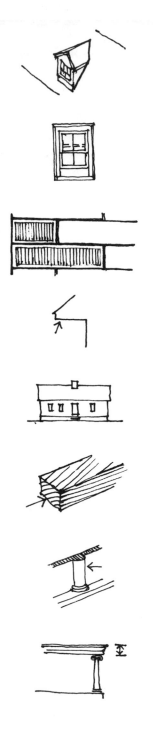

Entasis Outward swelling on a column to prevent the optical illusion that the column is narrowed at the middle

Façade The front of a building

Faceted Dormer Window Dormer window with more than one face, as in a bay window

Fanlights Window over a door which is fan-shaped, usually Neo-Classical

Fascia a. Vertical face between mouldings
b. Board nailed to the ends of the rafters

Fillet Top moulding in a cornice

Finial Ornament, e.g. fixed to the peak of an arch

Floor level Usually the finished top surface of a floor so that references are clear, e.g. basement

Fluting Grooves, in columns or in mouldings as decoration

Frame Originally the carpentry jointed rigid skeleton on which cladding was hung, later becoming any rigid structure [e.g. in steel, reinforced concrete or wood, no matter how the joints are made]

Fretwork Ornamental shapes cut by the thin-bladed fret saw. The decoration may be used in silhouette or applied flat

Frieze Moulding in the entablature, may be flat or carved

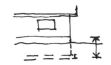

Foundation The lowest part of a building which transmits the weight into the ground

Gable Triangular part of an end wall to a pitched roof

Gambrel roof Roof with two slopes, the lower one of steeper pitch

Giant order An order used the full height of the wall

Glass block Unit made from two cast glass trays, bonded at the edges to form a hollow brick, which can be built as a wall

Glazing bar Rabbeted wood or metal support to hold glass

Glazing, double Two panes of glass separated by a cavity and sealed at the edges to provide improved thermal resistance

Greenhouse A glass walled and roofed space for plants

Half-timbering A frame of wood with infill so that the frame is exposed. In Europe the frame is often dark against a light infill and sometimes the patterns are ornate, with extra wood used to provide bracing

Half-hipped roof Roof with truncated gables

Hip or hipped roof Roof shape with slopes on all sides

Ionic One of the styles of Orders

Jamb Vertical posts in a door or window frame

Joist Floor support beam

Keystone The top and last stone to be put into an arch, sometimes decorated

Kneewall A wall of incomplete height, either between attic floor and rafter or at foundation level between top of foundation wall and ground floor joists

Lean-to Shelter with a single slope roof

Lintel Horizontal wood or stone beam over an opening, such as a window or door

Loggia An open gallery, often pillared

Mansard Double sloped roof shape named after the French architect François Mansart (1598-1666)

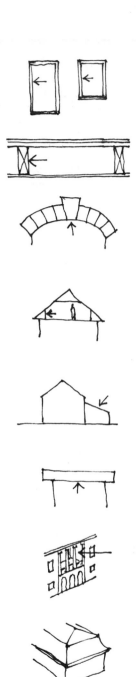

Masonry Originally stone and the art of building with it. Now includes building with brick and concrete block

Medallion A circular decoration

Module Dimensional unit to facilitate planning and construction. In classical architecture it was related to the diameter at the base of a column which established all the other dimensions of the building

Mortar Material used to join bricks and stone in masonry

Moulding Relief decoration, with contours having specific relationships to one another

Muntin The vertical member in a door, between the stiles. It is often incorrectly used to name a glazing bar.

Open plan The elimination of interior walls to give a continuity of space

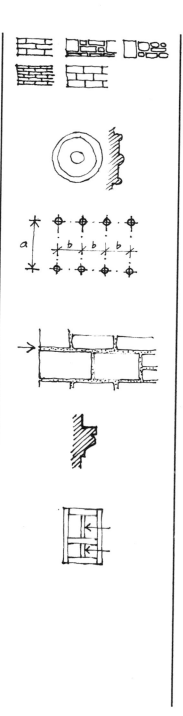

Orders In classical architecture the complete system of column and moulding making up the façade of a building. The Doric order on the Parthenon in Athens is an example. Other orders are Ionic, Corinthian, Tuscan and Composite

Oriel A bay window supported by brackets

Overhang Projection of a roof, floor etc.

Palladian Often applied to the shape of a window used by Andrea Palladio (1508-1580)

Panel Unit within a frame

Pantile Clay tile with simple overlaps

Parapet A low wall at the edge of a balcony or roof

Parging Thick external plaster, often patterned with castings

Pavilion Either a separate building or an accentuated part of a larger façade

Pedestal The base of a column

Pediment The triangular gable of a classical temple

Pendant Hanging decoration

Pilaster A portion of wall thickened for stability or as an ornament and often given similar mouldings to fit an Order

Pitch (of a roof) Angle of a slope usually given as a ratio of rise to going, 45% being 1:1 or 12" rise to 12" horizontal going

Plinth Thickening at the base of a wall

Podium A base

Porch A covered entrance to a building

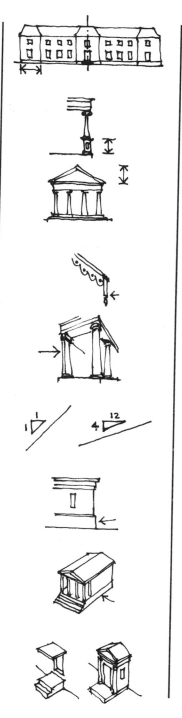

Porte Cochere A canopied entry, originally for carriages

Post and beam A type of construction, the main units of any framed construction and especially the combination of columns, laminated beams and thick decking built of Western Red Cedar

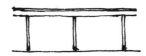

Portico Porch with columns and pediment

Prefabricated Made away from, but assembled on, the construction site

Purlin Horizontal roof member spanning between rafters, originally developed to support thatch roofing

Quoin Thickened blocks at the corner of a masonry wall

Rafter Major wood framing members in a roof, spanning between the wall and ridge

Rail In a frame, such as a door, window sash or panel, the horizontal members, usually mortise and tenon jointed to the vertical stiles

Relief Three-dimensional texture or projection

Return A moulding or pattern which continues round a corner

Reveals The side of a window or door opening between the outer wall surface and the door or window

Rococo The style of the High Baroque, especially the free flowing asymmetrical decoration

Rustication In masonry, the exaggeration of the joints and the roughness of the stones, usually at the base of a wall

Salt box A term used in New England to describe a house form generated by a two-storey house with an attached addition roofed from the ridge to a single storey. The shape is reputed to resemble an eighteenth-century salt box

Sash A glazed frame—fixed, sliding or hinged

Scale a. Proportion used in determining relationships of dimensions
b. A subjective judgement of apparent size

Shingles Small pieces of wood split or sawn, nailed over one another as a rainproof finish

Shutter External or internal, solid or slatted window cover

Sill Bottom member of a door or window frame

Soffit The underside of an overhang

Solar From the sun, as in passive solar heating

Spandrel The area of wall outside an arch but within the lines drawn vertically and horizontally from it

Split level Particular form of house where the living room is located at the half-way point between the upper and lower levels

Stile In a frame, the perimeter vertical framing members, often referred to in doors as the hinge stile or the meeting stile

Stone Building material of natural cut rock, e.g. granite

Stoop Large step, open or covered; a Dutch verandah

Storey The height, floor to floor at any level

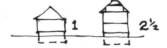

String course A flat projecting band of masonry, usually at a floor level

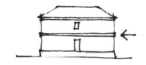

Stucco Plaster used on the exterior over wood or masonry

Stud frame Vertical light wood posts nailed to a sill at the bottom and a plate at the top to form a wall. Unlike masonry it is both quick and light

T & G boarding Boards shaped with a tongue on one edge and a groove on the other so that they can be fitted together without gaps

Temple front The wall and gable in Greek Revival where the front has been placed at the end of the form

Thatch Roofing material of overlaid bundles of reed or straw

Tile Usually a thin burned clay plate for roof, floor or wall covering

Tower Vertical form, usually attached to the front of a house to add weight and strength to the composition

Tracery Decorative shapes of glazing bars in Gothic Revival window openings

Transome or transom The horizontal frame member between a door and the windows above it, hence transome window above the door

Trim Small wood sections used as casings, picture rails or simple decoration

Truncated Cut off or cut short

Tuscan One of the styles of Orders

Venetian blind Type of adjustable window blind which allows control over the amount of light admitted

Ventilator Fixed opening with fly screen and rain protecting louvres, usually prefabricated of metal

Verandah Covered porch or balcony

Vestibule Covered and enclosed entry to a building

Voussoir The wedge-shaped stones used to build an arch

Guide to Buildings

Elements

In trying to determine the style of a house it is sometimes easier to focus on one element at a time, by selecting a detail and tracking down its likely date or style, making quick comparisons.

The task of breaking down a complex whole into manageable parts to simplify it for better understanding introduces the need to isolate those elements that are most descriptive of the whole or that are most easily discerned. There will probably be a change in attitude as the observer develops a taste for the individual components, but for most people it is likely that the larger elements will be seen first and the details will be secondary. The elements have therefore been listed in approximate order of size or visual impact: Form, Elevation, Door, Window, Construction and Decoration.

Elements

Form

Elevation

Door

Window

Construction
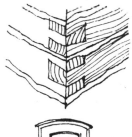

Decoration

Form

Form is the three-dimensional shape of an object. It comes about by combining the plan configuration and the number of stories. A significant influence on form is how the building meets the ground, the floor level to ground level relationship, and the height of steps, terraces or porch. The primary features of form include the plan shape, the roof shape and the location of the chimneys. Other elements that, though secondary, have considerable visual impact, such as towers, small extensions, porches, balconies and verandahs may have a major impact on the form.

A house may comprise attached forms, stretching back from a house facing the road to a barn at the back. In between house and barn are a number of extensions as kitchen, washhouse, shed, woodshed and outhouse. In many cases the complete composition was built at the same time, but the appearance is of a gradual accretion of forms over time.

One of the primary descriptive elements is the roof. It is not only a significantly visible element, but is subject to great variety of treatment according to the whims of fashion. Most noticeable is the direction of the ridge, either parallel to the road or at right angles to it. The ability to reduce the steepness of the pitch, and still make the roof waterproof, has generated a very different set of conditions for the form. To begin with it was technically difficult and expensive to make flat roofs, but later technical advances resulted in a freedom of expression that was to generate not only roofs of various pitches, but also roofs that combined different slopes. Later still roofs used curves in both plan and section and were covered with wooden shingles.

Chimney locations and mass are easily spotted from a distance. Initially the chimney breast was massive and central, or in larger houses was split into two inner cores. Later houses used decentralized chimneys, even perimeter ones. With the introduction of the enclosed stove, the chimney became much smaller, sometimes not even supported on the ground, but on an upper floor. After World War Two chimneys were even placed outside the house wall, wasting heat to the exterior.

Form

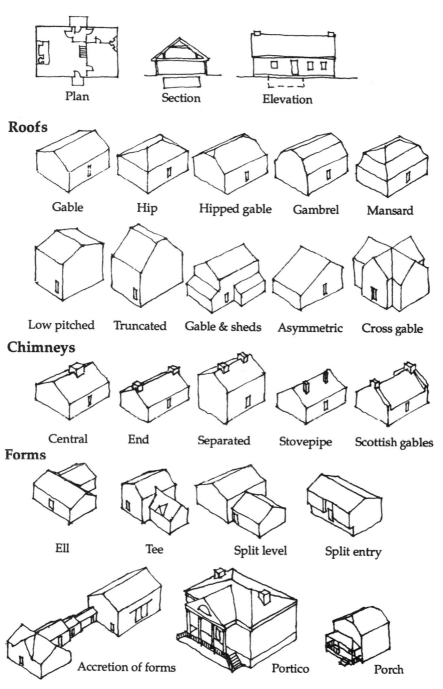

Plan Section Elevation

Roofs

Gable Hip Hipped gable Gambrel Mansard

Low pitched Truncated Gable & sheds Asymmetric Cross gable

Chimneys

Central End Separated Stovepipe Scottish gables

Forms

Ell Tee Split level Split entry

Accretion of forms Portico Porch

Elevation

When we look at a house, what we see is usually an elevation or else two sides in perspective. The elevation holds most of the clues to the style. In the elevation the wall is shown relative to the roof and to the ground. The wall is a significant part of the elevation in that it shows the true scale of the parts and their relationship to one another: it describes in very simple yet clear terms the proportions, balance, symmetry or asymmetry of the composition, and the image of the whole. Symmetry is normal to the classical styles and asymmetry to the romantic styles, but there is plenty of middle ground where the style is neither one nor the other. The elevation is where we see this most clearly.

One aspect of scale and image is the relationship between the ground level and the floor level inside, which is most clearly shown in elevation. Entry via steps is a very different experience to entry on the level, and most buildings endeavouring to achieve an imposing image use steps as the first stage. Scale is a difficult design component to master. It is dependent not only on the actual size of the wall and the openings but also on the apparent size. The elevation may pretend to be a house and actually be a cottage.

Another significant factor in the elevation and how we read it is the solid-to-void ratio, that is, the amount of wall to opening. In early houses the proportion is likely to be a lot of wall to a little window, whereas in modern houses the proportion is more likely to be even. The great difference between a wall with substantially vertical openings and one with horizontal openings has to be seen to be believed; the change in image is dramatic even when the windows are of the same size.

On a smaller scale, the texture and pattern in the wall itself as well as in the components of the wall, such as the windows, have considerable impact on the way we see a house. Over time, siding materials have been reduced in width, or in apparent width.

Elevation

Elements

Roof
Cornice
Roof
Dormer window

Cornice

Wall
Corner trim
Window

Trim
Foundation

Storey height

1

1 ½

2

Scale

Small   Medium   Large

Composition

Horizontal   Vertical   Symmetry-almost

Asymmetry   Symmetry

Door

A significant point in the elevation is the entry, especially the front door. Attention may be increased by enhancing the decoration around the door. In some cases the door takes on the role of establishing the whole image of the house, and in other cases the door virtually disappears as it is enveloped and overshadowed by a porch roof or verandah. In later Victorian styles, like the Queen Anne Revival, a small pediment is often added to the front edge of the porch roof to attract attention back to the location of the entry because the door cannot be seen when well hidden in the shadows.

Steps and windows may radically alter the appearance of the door and its overall physical dimension although the actual opening remains the same size. Recent taste has encouraged the use of two doors, although one leaf is never used.

The common feature of Halifax doorways is the porch with lots of glass, and this is a rather delightful addition to any elevation. But why did it become so fashionable? It seems that protection from the weather was only partially responsible and that there may also have been a desire to allow the neighbours to see just who was coming to visit.

Not only are there a number of combinations of door and window configurations, but there are a number of door types as well. The idea that the door was the weak point in the wall, that it had to be both solid and studded to resist axe blows, was forgotten by the time of the Victorian glazed door. One may even find the glass coloured, or engraved or sand- blasted with the initials of the owner.

Sometimes with three different numbers on the one house, the history if not the change in style can be read directly. Doorknobs, letter flaps, bell pushes and nameplates are less important accessories than house numbers. Light fittings associated with the door may have an impact far beyond what might be expected. The use of the carriage lamp, much in favour at the moment, is an example where fashion adds an element of make-believe to an ordinary wall light.

Doors

Elements

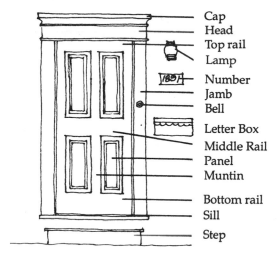

- Cap
- Head
- Top rail
- Lamp
- Number
- Jamb
- Bell
- Letter Box
- Middle Rail
- Panel
- Muntin
- Bottom rail
- Sill
- Step

Types

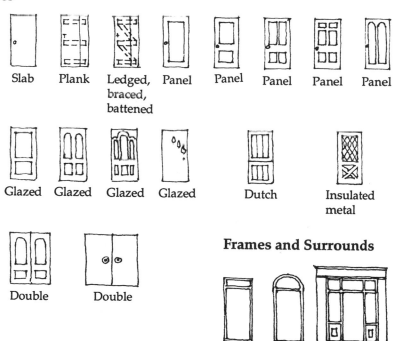

| Slab | Plank | Ledged, braced, battened | Panel | Panel | Panel | Panel | Panel |

| Glazed | Glazed | Glazed | Glazed | Dutch | Insulated metal |

| Double | Double |

Frames and Surrounds

Window

Possibly because most houses are equipped with so many windows, they are a major influence on the look of a house. Not only are their size and shape important, but so are their mechanisms for holding the glass, allowing ventilation, providing protection from weather and reducing heat loss. Developments in the manufacture of glass have increased the usable size of the pane and because we know the chronology of these developments, we have a method of dating windows. Other window details worth noting include the style of moulding separating the individual panes of glass, the proportion of the frame, and the type of decorative surround.

The large-scale variations in the shape and disposition of the openings in a wall appear to be more important than the type of window itself. This is probably due to the way we take in the information. At a distance we *read* the elevation and take from it the information we need to give us a first impression, to answer such questions as "Is this the front of the house?" It is only later that we might notice that the front door has a peculiar window above it.

Storm windows have often been added to windows in such a way that the original window shape and pattern of glazing is hidden from view. The appreciation of the style of a house may be dramatically altered by these additions. Care must be exercised to ensure that the real window is being studied and that even this is real. Beware the influence continual maintenance may exert on the slow change of the clues. For example, old window frames may have been scraped and repainted several times, each scraping modifying the shape of the moulding.

As with doors, window surrounds are liable to decoration, and much can be learned from an inspection of a window from the inside. The emphasis of this book is on exteriors: observe how additions like shutters may dramatically alter the appearance of the window without changing the real style at all. Neither window boxes for flowers nor awnings will alter style, but they make a vast difference to the appearance.

Window

Elements

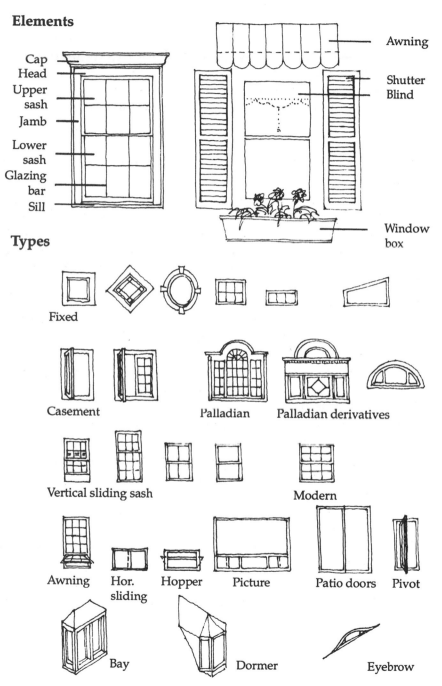

Cap
Head
Upper sash
Jamb
Lower sash
Glazing bar
Sill

Awning

Shutter
Blind

Window box

Types

Fixed

Casement   Palladian   Palladian derivatives

Vertical sliding sash   Modern

Awning   Hor. sliding   Hopper   Picture   Patio doors   Pivot

Bay   Dormer   Eyebrow

Construction

The relationship of the wall to the roof, of the wall to the foundation and of the wall to the openings in it, may all derive from the wall materials and how they are used. The actual means of building are usually hidden from view in the thickness of the wall or lost above the ceiling. Many walls clad on the exterior with shingles are actually solid log walls, and some that appear to be stone are merely painted wood plank with stone dust added to the paint. It goes without saying that houses that have been altered and upgraded, so-called renovated, can be misleading to the style hunter at first glance.

Today the size of windows is neither limited by the technology available to glass manufacturers, nor by structural elements such as the spacing of the studs or the size of the bricks in the wall. Prefabrication to standard measurements makes for predictable costs. Economic lengths of timber, economic depths of floor joists and economic spacing of the joists to reduce the bounce in the floor are hardly apparent on the exterior, yet these influences are all there in the design of the elevation. Standardization of dimensions based on the width of sheets of plywood and plaster board has also become common.

Perhaps the greatest change in the construction of houses during the last few years has come from the development of new finishes, such as the plastic coatings now being used instead of paints and the various cladding materials that speed the enclosure of a new house. But another recent change of some magnitude is the development of standard large components, such as roof trusses and wall panels. It is important to remember that standardization is not new, it has been with us for a long time, especially in the overall sizes of houses and in the sizes of doors and windows. In the eighteenth century there were even standard sizes of hearths, although they were made of small bricks and could have been of many sizes.

Examining the relationship of material to dimensions may reveal much about the ancestry of a building.

Construction

Materials (influence on exterior)

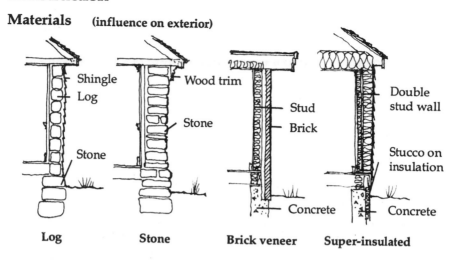

- Shingle
- Log
- Stone

Log

- Wood trim
- Stone

Stone

- Stud
- Brick
- Concrete

Brick veneer

- Double stud wall
- Stucco on insulation
- Concrete

Super-insulated

Materials (influence on external appearance)

Stone

Brick

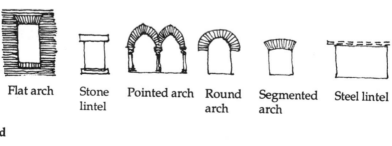

Flat arch   Stone lintel   Pointed arch   Round arch   Segmented arch   Steel lintel

Wood

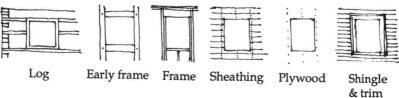

Log   Early frame   Frame   Sheathing   Plywood   Shingle & trim

Decoration

At first sight we may assume that the whole idea of style is tied up in the decorative elements of the house, and that other elements are subsidiary to decoration. But it is soon obvious that this is not the case: all the components of the house have their individual roles to play in making a style.

Decoration, apparently being the easiest part of a house to alter, is the least stable part of the house. It must be recognized that the trim so lavishly added to Late Victorian houses was highly susceptible to rot, corrosion and weathering and, in many cases, has suffered badly and been removed in part or in whole. As a result, the style value of the decorative elements has sometimes been lost. It is significant that however decoration is removed it is seldom stripped off to be replaced by an alternative style of decoration. This is really rather heartening in that the integrity of the design somehow appears to be apparent to the general public.

Unlike the parts of the building that are integral to the construction and stability of the structure, decoration can utilize many techniques. The development of various mechanical means of producing mouldings had a direct effect on the amount of trim used in a house. The thoughtless use of trim today may in part be due to its general availability.

Perhaps the most remarkable notion about style is that it is visible and discernable even in the smallest piece of trim, as well as in the colour of the paint or the overall shape of the roof.

The implications for style are intriguing as the pace of change in styles is increasing at the same time that the building industry is trying to make materials last longer. In future there may be less incentive to change styles when paint is not available to affect the changes because the materials could all be permanently self-coloured.

Decoration

Entablature

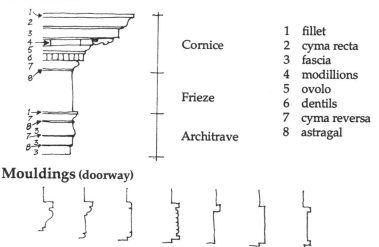

Cornice
Frieze
Architrave

1 fillet
2 cyma recta
3 fascia
4 modillions
5 ovolo
6 dentils
7 cyma reversa
8 astragal

Mouldings (doorway)

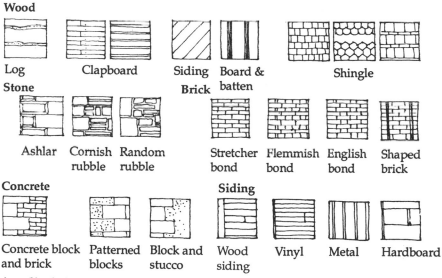

Inherent decoration (textures and patterns of material)

Wood

Log   Clapboard   Siding   Board & batten   Shingle

Stone   **Brick**

Ashlar   Cornish rubble   Random rubble   Stretcher bond   Flemmish bond   English bond   Shaped brick

Concrete   **Siding**

Concrete block and brick   Patterned blocks   Block and stucco   Wood siding   Vinyl   Metal   Hardboard

Applied decoration

Fretwork   Butterfly

Bracket   Baluster   Dormer   Finial

Styles

1605-1756

French

When the Sieur de Monts settled his band of fur traders on the north shore of the Annapolis Basin in 1605, the style of building was that of his homeland. Destroyed in 1613 and reconstructed in the 1930s, the complex is now called Port Royal Habitation. It was the first known European housing in Nova Scotia that can once again be seen and assessed.

Fortress Louisbourg was started in 1713, captured by the British in 1745 and in 1758, and was finally demolished by the British Army in 1760. Partially rebuilt in the 1970s, it shows a later stage in the transfer of an architecture from France to North America.

In both Port Royal and Louisbourg there are unmistakable French qualities in the shapes of roofs, openings, arches, windows and doors, and casement windows. The designs travelled as drawings from France and in the minds of the men who built them.

Louisbourg is interesting today as an example of the way that architectural style travels. The military buildings were designed in Paris and funds were supplied to permit their construction, but the civilian buildings used traditional French methods modified for the Canadian climate. When reconstruction began, the original drawings of military buildings were found carefully filed in Paris. This meant that extraordinary fidelity has been achieved in the reconstruction. The civilian buildings designed on the spot were reconstructed from archaeological and graphic evidence.

In present-day Louisbourg we find a superb example of reconstruction from ground level upwards of part of the original town. The method of building is often clearly expressed on the outside of the houses, but we need to interpret what we see with care. The reconstruction is probably much better built than the original and it is most probable that the buildings were quickly dilapidated.

Hipped or gable-ended roofs tend to have a pitch steeper than 45 degrees. They often have a bell curve at the eaves.

Louisbourg (R)

Asymmetry is common in the smaller houses, with a characteristic high wall, small dormer windows and tall windows. The timber wall framing may show externally.

c 1730 Louisbourg (R)

Doors vary in shape according to the wall material but typically are rectangular in wood frame and arched in stone walls. Shutters tend to be full height and solid.

Louisbourg (R)

Windows are normally casement type, hinged to swing inwards when shutters are used on the exterior.

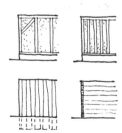

Louisbourg (R)

Construction methods in wood vary considerably, even in the walls. The main types are (a) widely spaced frame posts, with stone, wood or mud infill; (b) narrow spaced frame posts or studs, with infill; (c) vertical logs erected in a trench; and (d) horizontal logs squared and dovetail jointed at the corners.

Louisbourg (R)

1605-1755

Acadian

In 1755 Governor Lawrence of Nova Scotia ordered the expulsion of the Acadian people from the province of Nova Scotia and the destruction of their buildings, crops and livestock. This was an attempt to ensure loyalty to the British Crown by all the inhabitants of the province and to leave no reason at all for anyone unwilling to swear allegiance to the Crown to return to Nova Scotia. Out of 10,000 Acadians it is thought that 5,000 were transported to destinations in the southern colonies and that some were sent to France, while many removed themselves to isolated areas of the region. A considerable number of Acadians remained and built and farmed under British military supervision. In theory all their buildings were destroyed between 1755 and 1763. It is only very recently that extant Acadian or French houses have been found incorporated into other buildings in Annapolis Royal. These date from about 1710 and give some insight into the nature of Acadian building construction.

An Acadian house site in the Annapolis Valley has been investigated by archaeologists from the Nova Scotia Museum, and large amounts of clay were found during the excavations. The clay appears to have been used as an interior wall finish, not unlike thick plaster. The house was bigger than expected and suggests a better standard of living than had been assumed previously, and a strong New England influence.

The Acadians became renowned for their squared log construction with dovetailed corners. As few of these houses can be definitely attributed to Acadian craftsmen or designers, we have to rely on a few illustrations of Acadian buildings and the two houses built in Annapolis Royal. The excavated sites indicate the size and materials of these buildings, but we have no known examples of doors or windows or external wall finish existing today.

There are only two known Acadian houses still standing, dating from before 1755, but both are much altered. The house investigated by Museum archaeologists had a brick bake-oven located adjacent to the chimney and a shelter for animals at the other end of the house.

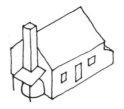

Belleisle (D)

The squared log house is small and may have shingles hiding the wall material. Walls are high and the ends of upper floor joists may be visible on the outside. The roof spaces were used for storage so attic windows were not required.

Weymouth (D)

Original doors are very unlikely to still exist, except possibly internally.

Although casement windows would be expected, it seems that many windows were fitted with vertical sliding sashes at an early date, possibly as a symbol of cultural assimilation.

Annapolis Royal

Wall construction is either of solid wood as horizontal log, or may be of frame with mud or stone infill. In either case it seems likely that shingles were used on the outside to resist rain penetration.

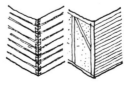

1749-1830

Neo-Classical
Finding an acceptable name for this style in Nova Scotia is difficult. Several names have been used over the years but none is truly satisfactory. Late Baroque is too flamboyant a style, implying Rococo. Classic Revival is usually reserved for the next appearance of the style in the early nineteenth century. Palladian assumes that all the designs are variations on this Italian architect's works, which they are not. In the United Kingdom it is commonly known as Georgian and includes the later subtle refinements of Regency. In the United States it is known as Georgian for buildings built before 1776 and, after Independence, as Federal style. Its period both precedes and extends beyond the reigns of the four Georges. Neither Queen Anne nor early-Victorian styles are easily distinguished from it. To further complicate the issue, most houses referred to as Georgian style in North America are grand, whereas in any period the common buildings are lumped together under the term Vernacular architecture. For clarification, the styles of this period in the context of Nova Scotia are best termed Neo-classical derivations, or Neo-classical for short.

No matter what name is used, there is a wide range in architectural styles within the Neo-classical period in England, Scotland, the West Indies, tidewater Virginia and New England. These major influences on the architecture of Nova Scotia, both grand and humble, can still be found. Other terms that further confuse this period and are not used in this book are as follows: Cape Cod, which is too restrictive and reflects unique limits to time, location and design; Colonial, which is far too broad a term covering a 200-year period and several styles; and Planter, which is a term for a type of settler rather than for an architectural style, the same as Loyalist refers to a political refugee.

Early in the reign of George II, the architectural works of Andrea Palladio were republished in London and were immediately copied. This was followed during the reign of George III by Stuart and Revett's publication of the first volume of their work on ancient Greek architecture, which immediately influenced the rigour with which the classical orders and decorations were used.

Much archaeological digging of ancient monuments and a growth in scholarship resulted in many books of measured drawings in which the "Orders" were explained and the actual proportions were stated and refined. This generated a new style—Neo-classical. Thus, the architecture in Britain from about 1730 to 1830 was greatly influenced by two books and many interpreters who in turn published many pattern books. Over 100 such books were in use in North America before the American Revolution.

In Nova Scotia it is extremely difficult to discern the subtleties. Many of the houses are small, and the strongest influence appears to come from New England craftsmen rather than from the pattern books or directly from Britain. In the larger houses, of which so few remain, some classical influences are very obvious—Uniacke House is a good example.

Standards of craftsmanship were high, and pattern books were universally available. Whether for large or small houses, the Neo-classical style involved symmetry, vertical sliding sash windows, some degree of classical proportion, mouldings based on historic models and often a doorway with some reference to an ancient building. Even cottages, which were not necessarily symmetrical nor had a pediment at the door, maintained the same mouldings as could be found in classical antiquity.

There are not many examples of Neo-classical buildings in Nova Scotia. This may be due to economic factors as this was the period of early settlement in the province. Even though some Georgian houses were built, many have been replaced, removed, altered or destroyed by fire.

Between 1713 and 1815, wars and threats of war were never far away, and investment was never without risk. Most houses of the period were modest and built of wood. Throughout the province the moderate to small-scale houses were built on well-developed principles that were clearly influenced by British and North American prototypes, but they had developed out of the medieval styles common to the original colonial settlers. The roofs were in the style of the previous century. A minor influence can be seen in houses built by Loyalists of Dutch descent, where a bellcast is evident in the roof. The Scottish influence is more noticeable in raised gable ends and shaped dormer windows than in the use of stone for walls. Because of the number of examples of Scottish houses, these are discussed in a separate category.

Despite the different directions of the architectural influences, the remarkable characteristic of the Neo-classical style is its longevity. This may have been a subconscious reaction to the continual stress of war. It is not surprising that an architecture built by hand was resistant to change. Tools were made by their owners and lasted a lifetime. Houses were built by men whose apprenticeships lasted seven years. Hard-earned skills were not the material of rapid change; even so, it is worth noting how refined the Neo-classical style became at its peak.

This was the time when refugees—Loyalists—were arriving in Nova Scotia. These were often wealthy urban dwellers, and one of the plans for resettlement was the growth of Shelburne. By 1783 this South Shore town had the third largest population of any town in the New World and could boast some very fine houses. Unfortunately this effort was not successful and within five years the population had decreased dramatically. Empty houses were used as firewood. The grand scale of the original plans is still visible in the street patterns rather than in the buildings themselves, although some are still there to tell the tale of Shelburne's prosperous days.

Larger buildings of this period were sponsored by the government and tended to be designed in Britain and built in Nova Scotia. However, the first Lieutenant-Governor's residence was prefabricated in Boston for erection in Halifax.

Variations in style arrived as quickly as the boat could transport a book or drawing from London to Halifax. It is remarkable how rapidly fashion was transferred, even to an outpost of the Empire such as Nova Scotia. The universal style in form, window and door mouldings did not limit development. Rather, the pattern books established rules. Halifax's Town Clock and St. George's Church demonstrate this, as both exhibit a free intellectual interpretation for round buildings. But change was not the rule to live by. When Simeon Perkins extended his house twenty-six years after building the first phase, he carried on in the same style. When Richard John Uniacke built his country house in 1813, the design he used was almost identical to that of a house in Manhattan that had been built sixty years earlier.

Neo-classical was both the founding style for the new colony and the longest lasting of all the architectural styles discussed in this book.

Single Storey

Here is the universal solution to the small house, which is still being copied. The original model was built for over a century in New England. Note the fat central chimney, small overhangs of the roof and less than 45- degree pitch to the roof.

Symmetry was normal, but many variations exist that must have been original. Because of their age many of these houses have been modified over time, tending to be lengthened to an asymmetrical face.

Doors are not likely to be original, but check the hinges and locks. Panelled doors tend to be of fine craftsmanship. Fanlights and transom lights are always small in the smaller houses but can be very large in the bigger ones.

Windows are usually vertical sliding and many appear rather large in comparison to the house. An uneven number of vertical panes is quite common, making the sashes of unequal height. Trim is often very simple and glazing bars delicate.

Construction is refined to a large degree, with frames sometimes visible inside but always prefabricated prior to final assembly. Hence the Roman numerals incised at the pegged joints.

Details vary little. Main changes are in the amount of projection rather than in the mouldings. Corner trim is slim, and cornice returns on the gable ends are short.

1786 Mill Village

1786 Mill Village

1767 Liverpool

1767 Liverpool

1767 Liverpool

1767 Liverpool

Multi-Storey

Although rarer than single-storey houses, two-or three-storey houses do exist. Some are remarkably large, like Government House in Halifax.

1819 Halifax

Symmetry is the rule, and in the wooden houses is apparent even in the central chimney. Porches have very often been added.

c 1800 Avonport

Doors may be extremely elegant. This one is intermediate, with simplified mouldings, but retain at least a trace of elegance.

c 1800 Halifax

This triple window was less common than the single window. It is not very common in Nova Scotia. A few of the fashionable Palladian window shapes are used, such as the semi-circular, but the most commonly related Palladian window, with three parts, the centre round arched, tends to be seen more in churches than in houses until a century later. (See *Queen Anne Revival*)

c 1821 Tatamagouche

Decoration is often subtle, but mouldings are used in combinations and proportions that have had historic precedent. The scale is always human and the mouldings delicate.

1785 Shelburne

Neo-classical Forms

Compared with the more typical house on the previous page, this one is symmetrical except for the one window and has less typical end chimneys. Simeon Perkin's house in Liverpool originally looked like this.

To build a smaller house was easy; just leave out one window bay. In New England this is referred to as a three-quarter house.

Even cheaper was a half-house! Few remain, as most were extended or altered soon after construction.

Houses of the "salt box" shape can be found, but they are less common than in New England. They appear to have been originally built this way in Nova Scotia and not created from additions.

Very few really grand houses were built in Nova Scotia, but a number of substantial two-storey houses have survived. The scale can be quite large, the chimneys massive, and the entrance hall grand and intended to impress.

Gambrel-roofed houses were once common but it seems that a disproportionate number have been destroyed, making them relatively uncommon today.

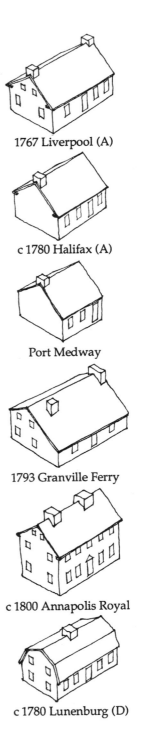

1767 Liverpool (A)

c 1780 Halifax (A)

Port Medway

1793 Granville Ferry

c 1800 Annapolis Royal

c 1780 Lunenburg (D)

Neo-classical Variations

It is remarkable how much variety can be generated within one style. In all these examples, symmetry is common but there are variations in the number of windows, the effective number of floors, the materials used in construction and the surface complexity.

At the top is a brick house that could easily have been built in England.

Below is a stone house designed in England.

This brick house has unusual flat arches over the central door and window.

This urban house had projecting bays on either side of a recessed entrance.

The rounded bays on this house cause the roof to sweep out. Notice the difference in the heights of the windows.

This now demolished house gives an idea of the wealth that was once here. This was the rear, or garden, elevation.

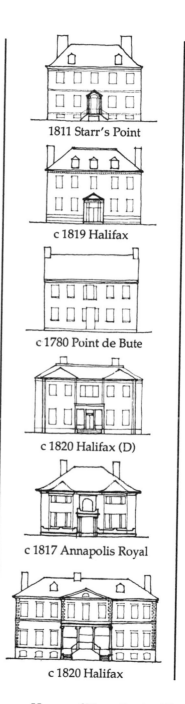

1811 Starr's Point

c 1819 Halifax

c 1780 Point de Bute

c 1820 Halifax (D)

c 1817 Annapolis Royal

c 1820 Halifax

1790-1840

Scottish

One group of immigrants that came to Nova Scotia with a highly refined variation of the Neo-classical style were the Scots. The number of their houses remaining to this day bears witness to the quality of the construction and, incidentally, to the design.

Those people who could afford to use stone built homes that are close copies of Scottish houses. This is most evident in the gable ends, where the wall extends up above the plane of the roof. The exposed top edge of the wall is always smooth, which suggests that most builders were from the west of Scotland. In the east of Scotland the gables are more often finished in a series of steps.

In the towns, the terrace houses provide a rare glimpse of the urban texture that these settlers left behind, with continuous stone walls facing the street as house follows house, all made safe in case of fire by the use of the stone for the dividing walls. Façades are usually of dressed stone, but the side and rear walls often turn out to be rough surfaced random or coursed rubble walls.

The other distinguishing element that is much more celebrated is the bay window in the dormer, often called a Scottish dormer. As many of these dormer windows were added to existing houses this element is not proof of Scottish ancestry! In the 1870s a book was published in Glasgow illustrating house designs. A cottage design that could have been found in Pictou has gable-end parapet walls and bay-windowed dormers. It is titled "A cottage in the Italian style." So much for style descriptions being helpful!

Classical influences can be seen in the symmetry, proportions, delicate trim and fine mouldings. Pictou is worth a visit to see the effect of a group of these houses which, despite their apparent severity, also convey a calm repose and sense of security.

Whether one or two storeys, the houses are simple yet elegant. Most noticeable is the raised gable wall, which comes directly from Scotland.

The general Neo-classical symmetry and simplicity is most evident in isolated houses but can also be seen in a few rows, notably in Pictou.

Doors are sometimes given the refinements of an Edinburgh townhouse, with all the detailed trim in fanlights and sidelights. It would be easy to believe that the designs originated with the Adam brothers.

The windows are invariably fine with thin glazing bars, set in minimal frames that contrast well with the stonework around them. These epitomize the elegance of the Neo-classical period.

Walls are usually of dressed ashlar stonework, with string course and plinth laid to project beyond the face of the wall.

The so-called Scottish Dormer has been adopted throughout the province, but the earliest ones were most likely built in Pictou and Halifax by Scottish craftsmen.

1805 Pictou

c 1825 Pictou

c 1850 Port Hood

1827 Pictou

1827 Pictou

c 1825 Pictou

1820-1860

Classic Revival

The Classic Revival style is epitomized in the Greek Revival, of which there is little in Nova Scotia to demonstrate its beginnings but much to show how rapidly it degenerated into a coarse and distant derivative of the original. Early Greek Revival forms and decoration grew out of the eighteenth-century desire for more accurate details based on archaeological studies of ancient buildings. In the newly formed United States the development of a style that clearly separated itself from a colonial past, and that alluded to an idealistic view of a new republic, began in Roman architecture and found its resolution in Greek Revival architecture.

Greek Revival became very popular in North America, but in "colonial" Nova Scotia it had to be tempered so as not to look too revolutionary. Because so many Nova Scotia examples would not be recognizable within the American or British Greek Revival styles, and because so many details are Roman as well as Greek, the style is more accurately called Classic Revival.

It was unfortunate that the style evolved just at the time when the province's economy fell apart, and so for a while there was little incentive to build at all, let alone in an untried style or one having explicit political overtones. As a result, we find the forms in Nova Scotia without the decoration or with partial decoration rather demurely included. The temple front never has its full Doric portico in Nova Scotia. Those buildings that demonstrate the style in Nova Scotia, like the Caldwell House (1840s) on Robie Street in Halifax, are rare.

In many cases there are a few Greek details, such as Ionic-columned porches, a row of horizontally emphasized windows in a frieze just below the eaves, or tall windows on the lower floor. Along with the style of building went paint of purest white.

The formality and refinements of the Greek Revival never reached the scale of the plantation buildings in the deep south of the United States. The few examples that remain in Nova Scotia stand alone: stark white against a dark forest or open sky.

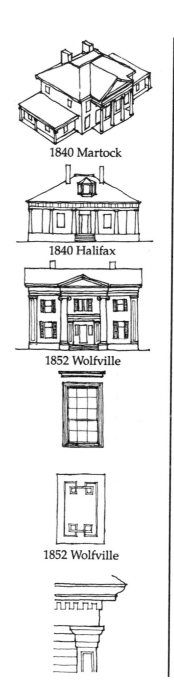

1840 Martock

Even the small houses are symmetrical and formal. Here the temple form is directly translated into a house with verandah, but with a hipped roof instead of a gable.

1840 Halifax

In this case, the scale is increased by the use of two-storey pilasters. And the Ionic order is correctly copied for the individual column, but not the spacing between the columns.

1852 Wolfville

Windows become much larger, with simple mouldings.

The fret motif is popular and is employed in many decorative elements, such as a panel beneath a window.

1852 Wolfville

Corners are often accentuated with wide pilasters, sometimes making the scale extremely large. In early cases, the mouldings are delicate and historically accurate, while later degenerating into heavy and crude approximations.

The Orders

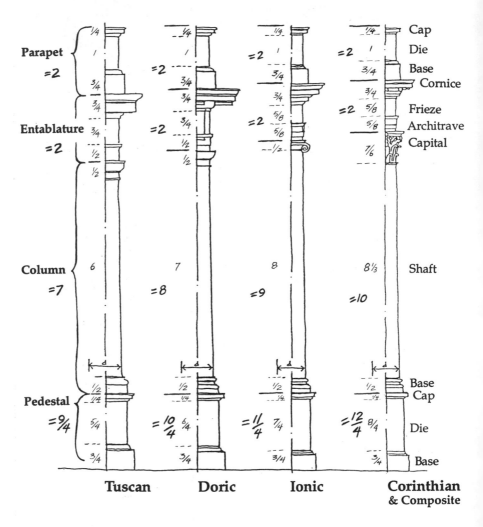

Tuscan Doric Ionic Corinthian
& Composite

After R.A. Cordingly

Note: all proportions are related to the diameter (d) at the base of the column, know as the module.

The "gable-end-to-the-road" house became very popular in the United States. The Nova Scotia house with a broken pediment developed out of a design that had a pediment forming the gable like the temples of antiquity. Nova Scotia has many houses with the form, but without the pediment.

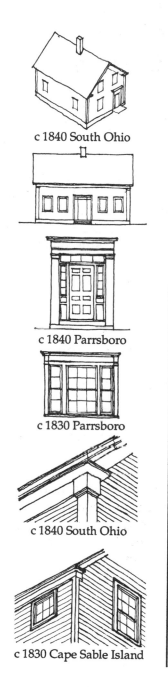

c 1840 South Ohio

The pronounced corner pilasters of the large houses are scaled down on the smaller ones.

As the style developed, the accuracy of the Neo-classical details was lost and simplified mouldings became common.

c 1840 Parrsboro

This Neo-classical window is made into Classic Revival by the simple addition of a cornice on the top and end pilasters.

c 1830 Parrsboro

Although originally celebrating greater authentic detail, the Orders were soon forgotten despite their ready availability in many pattern books. The crude simplifications lead to problems of scale.

c 1840 South Ohio

The rooms under the roof are lit by horizontal windows squeezed in below the eaves. They are sometimes so small that they are no more than ventilation slots.

c 1830 Cape Sable Island

1830-1890
Gothic Revival

Of all the styles of the Victorian era, Gothic Revival must be the best known and most easily recognized. Much happened, during its translation from the style adopted by the English intelligentsia in the mid-eighteenth century into the common style of Nova Scotia in the mid-nineteenth century.

The most obvious change is that a method of building so completely rooted in the stone from which it was painstakingly carved had to make a dramatic leap in technique when translated into wood. In his influential book, *The Architecture of Country Houses (1850)*, A.J. Downing writes that the house should be built in stone or stuccoed brick, or the wood should be painted a stone colour and have sand mixed into the paint to give it a stone texture.

Gothic Revival was used as an antidote to plain Neo-Classical derivatives. Ultimately it became the centre of an important ecclesiastical debate and was given credibility by the Church of England. But for most people it was a delightful change from the simple good proportions of the Neo-Classical and Classic Revival styles and gave the possibility of an acceptable romantic asymmetry, though seldom used this way in Nova Scotia houses. Given time it gradually defeated the Classic Revival style in housing and churches, and in parliament buildings, but is seldom associated with banks, which have remained staunchly Neo-Classical in style.

In the case of Nova Scotia, for the first time here was an architecture that apparently suited the climate. Greek architecture is ideally seen in the sunshine of a lower latitude. The steeply pitched roofs and delicate traceried porches or verandahs of the Gothic Revival were quite functional, and suited to heavy rain or snowfall.

The fundamental difference between the previous styles and the Gothic Revival is in the form. A cross gable is placed on the long side and it inevitably has a Gothic window, often of considerable size.

Lawrencetown

During the period of the style's development, the pitch of the roof increased. This is one indicator of age. Symmetry is normal.

1861 Sherbrooke

Doors and windows are generally the same as before, with a different trim. Classic Revival designs persist, especially at the front door.

Pointed windows are the hallmark. The variety is so great that a whole page has been devoted to the range of possibilities. It is common to make construction easier by straightening out the curved window frame.

Despite much enthusiastic writing by pattern-book authors, wall materials remained of clapboard or shingle with only a very few vertical board and batten examples in houses. There were, however, many more examples in churches.

Sherbrooke   Lockeport

The greatest fun for the observer is to hunt bargeboard designs. These are almost all the result of the power jig-saw and, in some cases, are flamboyant and grossly out of scale.

Some Gothic
Revival Bargeboards

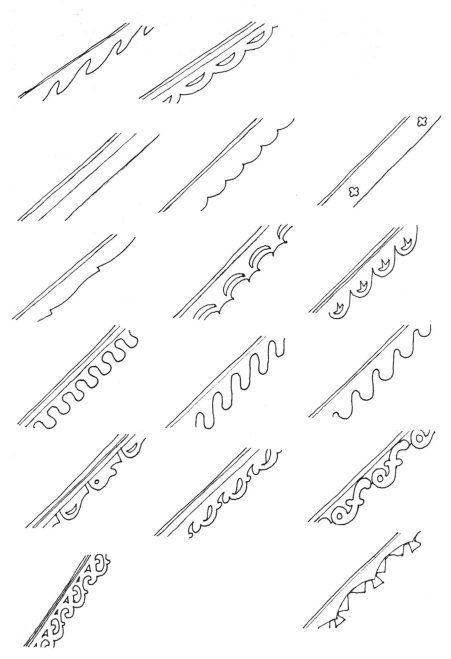

Gothic Revival Forms

The typical "small house" form is shown with single gable. In contrast to the previous styles where the eave trim returned onto the gable wall and there was a flat soffit, in Gothic Revival the soffit is usually sloping and continues up the gable ends.

An early example has a low pitch to the gable and a curved arch to the window.

Twin gables provide opportunity for another window but diminish the importance of the door.

This house is a mixture of the Classic Revival form and Gothic Revival details. The romantic asymmetry is commonly called Picturesque, which others have separated as a style on its own.

This three-gable house may originally have been a Neo-Classic or Classic Revival house because there are eave cornice returns on the gable ends. The projection of the centre bay is typical of later houses with three gables.

The end results of the style are shown here. The corners of the roof to the central bay have been cut off, the bay is faceted, and there are finials and pendants. All add complexity to form.

Gothic Revival
Windows

This is the true Gothic Revival pointed arch with its glazing bars modified so that it can be opened.

The curved arch was straightened to ease manufacture.

Late variations are far from the early ideas.

Hood mouldings could transform a rectangular window into one that was Gothic or even Palladian!

French Romanesque and Second Empire flavours can be sensed in this example.

1820-1900
Halifax House

The Halifax House is a style based on form, as it has incorporated many styles of decoration over its long lifetime. The plan and the form are more significant than the style of the ornamental details.

The typical house is three windows wide with an asymmetric front door, and is deep from front to back. To gain enough floor space within the limited frontage, the plan had to be deep, with the result that the roof became large at a relatively steep pitch. This was partially resolved by making the top of the roof flat. A good number have been built with masonry side walls, presumably for fire protection, and with wooden front and back walls.

Unlike their European contemporaries, Halifax Houses are built separately as detached buildings. In Europe they would have been linked together to form rows, terraces, squares and crescents. The Halifax House has one particular feature that relates to its origins, the so-called Scottish dormer. In Halifax the bay is normally straight sided with corners truncated at 45 degrees or less.

Typically the Halifax House has two storeys with attic and cellar and has been built close to the street line. Some doorways have since been given porches. A number of this type of house still exist, the earliest being of stone, then of shingle, and later of brick or stucco. The street façade is often treated as though the sides were to be hidden by adjacent buildings, and it is usually given a smooth surface with heavy quoins, whether built in stone or brick or stucco. If built of stone the street façade is frequently smooth ashlar with a projecting string course, and the sides of cheaper random rubble or coursed rubble.

The main impression is one of dour solidity and stability, which suited the original owners who were the principal merchants, professionals and officials in the province at the time.

This is really not an individual style, but more a form type. It seems to have originated as one house out of a terrace, with blank side walls.

The elevation is square and squat, and often the main floor is raised well above street level. Later, porches became very fashionable. (See *Italianate*)

Most decoration was placed at the front door in all the style variations, whether a porch was provided or not.

Windows fit the particular style, in this case Neo-classical.

The street façade is usually treated to a smooth ashlar finish, while the side walls are of cheaper, coursed rubble.

The dormer window is often a bay pattern, no matter the style of the rest of the house. In the later ones, however, there is unity of style with often extravagant outbursts at roof level.

c 1834 Hollis St.

c 1834 Hollis St.

c 1825 Morris St.

c 1825 Morris St.

Barrington St.

Spring Garden Rd. (D)

1850-1890

Italianate

Italian or Roman architecture had formed the basis for the architectural styles developed during the Renaissance in Northern Italy. The first major style that derived from this Italian influence in the nineteenth century was a picturesque form of modest town or country house design, usually called a villa. Later on the influence of the urban architecture of small Italian palaces was felt in a more formal Italianate style. Queen Victoria's Osborne House was Italianate. North American Italianate later spawned Bracketted.

Symmetry was the rule for smaller town houses and asymmetry with a tower for larger town or country houses. Generally there was a wealth of decoration in robust cornices incorporating heavily decorated brackets, which were often used in pairs. Windows were given more three-dimensional emphasis with bracketted hoods and even bracketted sills. In Nova Scotia the style is almost exclusively built in wood, giving at one end of the scale an impression of elegant taste and at the other end an impression of aggressive new wealth.

The originals were often built of stone covered in stucco, and the typical painting of yellow to red earth colours contrasted with the trim. Recently painted houses, where everything is white, lose much in the translation.

Roof pitch remained low until later when it started to merge into the Mansard roof of the slightly later French Second Empire style. At this point a gay abandon takes over, hinting at the riot of architecture known as Victorian Eclectic style. The reasons for the popularity of the more flamboyant late-Victorian styles may be seen in the context of Canada's history. Italianate and Confederation were contemporaries.

A small mansion is plucked from an Italian plain with a belvedere of dubious value in Nova Scotia.

c 1870 Halifax (D)

In contrast, the villa is based on a symmetrical plan with low-pitched roof and expressed rafters. The shape is very distinctive.

1854 Pictou

Some Halifax houses have Italianate porches with large expanses of glass. The window is modified Palladian and, as is often the case, is surrounded by ornate brackets and other applied decoration.

1872 Halifax

There are some masonry houses, especially in stucco, which have an easily recognized framing to the windows. The frame is narrowed on each side. The pair of semi-circular headed windows is a common feature.

1862 Halifax

Another porch with multiple-arched windows and low-pitched roof is the epitome of the later period.

Halifax

This porch, with its strong connections to northern Italy, has also a tinge of Byzantine. The growing influence of the machine on the construction industry is demonstrated by the free use of turned ornamental bosses.

1892 Halifax

1850-1890

Bracketted

Out of the Italianate style there developed a new style with less historical accuracy and considerably more vivacity—the Bracketted. The problem of trying to discuss style and discriminate between styles is probably hardest at this point, where Italianate changes into Bracketted. How do they differ from one another? In details! Although there may be paired brackets under Italianate cornices, the same detail in a Bracketted house will be coupled with rectangular windows rather than arched ones, and a doorway that is typically more Neo-classical.

It is also possible to find Bracketted houses in other basic forms and styles, such as Neo-classical or even Gothic Revival.

The most noticeable brackets are at the cornice or eaves, but others will appear at window and door heads and also under window sills. Generally brackets are paired, but may be single or in multiple clusters as well, always giving the appearance of supporting a heavy cornice or the ends of beams or rafters.

Bracketted style is perhaps as close as we ever get to a Baroque style in Nova Scotia. The brackets are usually vertical in shape, more like shelf brackets than the true Italianate where the bracket was the carved end of a projecting beam. As the eave projection increased, the necessity of support underneath became visually more desirable. One of the sad comments on the maintenance of these houses is that many of the brackets fail and are removed, leaving a top-heavy composition.

There is no particular form to this style, as it appropriated whatever was handy. Typically, brackets are paired, and as a derivative of the Italianate style, many houses have Italianate details.

c 1870 Shelburne

This is an example of a Classic Revival form, with Gothic gables and Bracketted details. Later on, the combinations become so muddled that the compote is called Eclectic.

c 1870 Lower East Pubnico

Simple mouldings are contrasted with large and often complex-shaped brackets holding up otherwise Classical architraves.

c 1870 Shelburne

Here a perfectly normal Neo-classical window is transformed by the paired brackets at each end of the architrave.

c 1870 Lower East Pubnico

A typical corner with paired brackets under the eaves illustrates that the brackets are each made up of three pieces of wood, the middle one being thicker and a bit smaller than the outer ones.

Knobs of turned wood are added as drop pendants.

1870 Maitland

1855-1900

Second Empire

When Napoleon III initiated the enormous extensions to the Louvre Palace in 1852, his architects chose to work in a style that was rooted in the French Renaissance. One of the features of the style was a roof with a steep slope at the eaves, topped by a low-pitched or flat roof. This is called a Mansard roof, after François Mansart (1598-1666), who used it in the chateau at Blois in 1635, although Pierre Lescot had previously used it in the original Louvre in 1551. The Mansard roof provides full headroom in the top storey.

The steeper slope of the roof may be straight, or straight with a bell curve, or curved, convex or concave. Finally, it was extravagantly ornate with a second cornice halfway up the slope. The top edge may have a cornice and may also have decorative metal trim of cast iron or wrought iron. A lot of the metal has disappeared through corrosion.

As a style, Second Empire later became very ornate and flamboyant. When reduced in scale from palace to house size a number of problems arise, chiefly with the dormer window. In houses, height is generally stretched by making the apparent wall stop at the cornice, which doubles as the window sill of the dormer windows. On occasion the wall is made higher, so the dormer window has to break through the cornice. In either case the dormer window can be highly decorated.

Another common feature is the use of the segmental arch or low arch in window and door openings. In the originals there would have been a considerable patterning of roof slates using different shapes and colours. Translated into Nova Scotian wood shingles, only the shape is sometimes decorated, though the steep slope is often painted which, according to whether the paint colour is of the wall or of the roof, may destroy the form.

Napoleon III was deposed in 1870, but the Second Empire style was used extensively for another 20 years in Nova Scotia and was especially popular in the French-speaking regions.

The roof is the main feature of Second Empire, with a wall terminating in a steeply sloping roof that is capped by a low-pitched hip or flat roof.

It is difficult to fit a dormer window into the curve of the steep roof, but the very nature of the style demands the dormers, and there are usually plenty of them.

Arched cornices are popular, often combined with brackets and lots of Classical detailing in the mouldings, which later degenerated into some remarkable shapes.

Windows are plain and simple or perhaps a little decorated. Invariably they have rounded tops, either semi-circular or segmentally arched. Window panes increase in size with improvements in glass manufacturing.

The clearest indicator of age within the style is the roof section, which progresses from simple and straight to complex and curved.

Dormer windows are given curved roofs, either segmental or semi-circular, or else follow the shape of the window and mouldings in elevation.

Shelburne

Halifax

Halifax

Shelburne

Shelburne

1860-1900
Lunenburg House

The Lunenburg House, like the Halifax House, is not really a style at all, but as a geographic variation is a sufficiently noteworthy architectural development to warrant separation from the eclectic late-Victorian period.

The distinctive feature of the Lunenburg House lies in its development of dormer windows. Often a faceted dormer window projects beyond the wall face and may form a porch for the front door. But it is in the roof of the dormer where the exuberance of decoration becomes truly remarkable; sometimes one or even two extra cornices are inserted in the roof slope to provide the utmost complexity. At first, Scottish dormer windows were added to existing Classic Revival houses. Over time, the dormers appear to have moved down the roof slope until they slipped over the edge and ultimately grew down to the ground. Later they grew up to form a tower, by which time the construction was integral with the house. Simple single roof designs were superseded in time by double and even triple roofs of amusing complexity.

There are signs of both Second Empire style and of a Late Bracketted/Gothic style in these Lunenburg houses. This rare specie is almost exclusively limited to Lunenburg County, with a few examples of Gothic porches in Sherbrooke Village and some examples as far away as Yarmouth County.

There may be a reason for this extravagant expression in Lunenburg. As the industrious population grew wealthier from the very serious business of fishing, they expressed themselves by investing in a little frivolity at home. The same prosperity that generated the large nineteenth century schooner fleet in the harbour also supported the porches and dormer windows on the land. The vivacity of the particular examples is remarkable and, in a relatively isolated region, must have been the work of only a few craftsmen.

As with the Halifax House, the Lunenburg House is not really a style but more a local dialect. The form bridges several styles and has many variations, often combining components from different styles.

The elevation is usually symmetrical and the shapes bold. Many of the houses were modified over time and consist of more than one style.

Porches can be very extravagant and ultimately incorporate Italianate motifs, with triple-arched openings and even door panels with arches at the top.

Window details vary with each style, but in the time span of porch development there tends to be some bracketting and embellishment. This includes some fretwork applied to panels at the end of the period.

In the sequence of development, the dormer window slid down the slope of the roof until it projected beyond its edge to form a canopy. Later it grew down to the ground to form an enclosed porch. By 1880 the dormer and porch were built as part of the whole and became grand.

1870-1910

French Romanesque Revival

The French Romanesque Revival style in North America appears to have begun with the American architect H.H. Richardson (1838-86), who trained as an architect in Paris. The writings of Viollet-le-Duc predate Richardson's training and may have been read by him before he returned to New England. Richardson's work appears to result from direct influences of existing buildings, especially those in the southwest of France.

Although French Romanesque was an influential style in the United States, the fully developed style is seldom seen in Nova Scotia. Instead, one easily recognized detail is rather commonly used—the round tower with a conical roof, usually located on a front corner. Both in France and in the United States the style is normally built with heavy rusticated stonework. In Nova Scotia it is usually translated into shingle walls with cornices in plain wood, sometimes with medallion ornamentation.

As another example of a revival of an historic style, this one is perhaps more romantic than many others, but in its translation to Nova Scotia the extraordinary medieval robustness of the original is usually lost in thin shingles. This apparent dichotomy between the form and the materials used to generate it creates an entirely new variation in the style in North America.

As the eclecticism of the later Victorian period developed, so the round tower and conical roof became a common feature, even invading the very English Queen Anne Revival style. Other shapes of tower, both octagonal and rectangular, were also used, usually with a bell cast roof and with as many sides to the pyramidal roof as there were sides to the tower.

There are relatively few pure French Romanesque style houses compared with those incorporating towers in the Late Victorian Eclectic style.

This is a rare example of a house of this style built of stone. Most such Nova Scotia houses are built of wood and shingles.

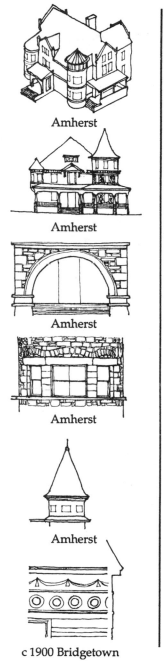

Amherst

The bartizan is an easily recognized clue to the style. In this example, a wood frame is clad with boulders at the round tower.

Amherst

Semi-circular arches are another trademark, especially when they rise from a low level.

Amherst

These windows in a circular stone tower show the dressed stone of the window surrounds and also the relieving arches above the lintels, which reduce the vertical load on the lintel.

Amherst

The most clearly recognized detail is the conical roofed tower. The walls are usually topped with a heavy Classical moulding that supports the roof, which often starts with a bell cast.

Amherst

A late tower moulding shows there is no rigour to the historicism. The decoration is determined by the availability of machined components from the local building supplier.

c 1900 Bridgetown

1880-1915
Queen Anne Revival

This is a curious style with several problems, the first of which is the name. When the Restoration took place in England in 1660, the royal family returned from Holland having been influenced by Dutch culture, especially in the use of brick. Sir Christopher Wren's architecture built on this base, and during the reign of Queen Anne a very considerable British style developed with large white painted wooden mouldings juxtaposed with red brick. Subsequently, the Neo-classical style developed to become the norm throughout the British Empire. During the nineteenth century, revivals of earlier styles followed one another in rapid succession until there seemed to be nothing left to revive. In England, Norman Shaw found a wholesomeness in the Queen Anne style that he revived in the 1870s with a succession of essentially English designs.

When the Queen Anne style was translated to North America it underwent a fundamental change. The clay tile hanging on the original walls was translated into wooden shingles, the parging became applied fretted wood, and the brickwork became a stud frame. As an architectural style ideally suited to country houses, it was used in Nova Scotia for a large number of private houses that all appear a little grand, whether in town or country settings, regardless of their true size.

In the translation to Nova Scotia there was a considerable paring down of decoration from the Norman Shaw originals, with only the main features remaining intact, including such details as bay windows with curved ends, Palladian windows and the shaping of the ends of the shingles. The original buildings of this style in Britain were all influenced by, or influential in, the Arts and Crafts movement.

There are many large houses built at the turn of the century with elements of Queen Anne Revival. The essentially simple form is usually camouflaged by a verandah. The gable end is always completed by a cornice to form a triangular pediment.

Later examples are hard to distinguish from other styles because so many parts are borrowed; always look though for Palladian windows, which are often located in the gable ends.

The Palladian window also appears in dormer windows, though in this late example it is heavily modified and partially hidden by an added storm window.

Again the Palladian window is used as a starting place and is treated to a considerable amount of development in three dimensions.

Shingle patterns became the rage with bands of patterns alternating up the wall. Although this originates with the style, the results are quite unlike anything that Queen Anne could have recognized. All this may now be hidden beneath new siding, which cannot copy the original.

Gable ends are often treated to a delightful display of originality by the builder and often incorporate curved walls and shaped shingles.

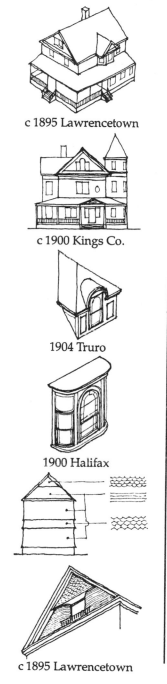

c 1895 Lawrencetown

c 1900 Kings Co.

1904 Truro

1900 Halifax

c 1895 Lawrencetown

Houses of Nova Scotia 85

1880-1910

Stick

Stick style is a name given to a late Victorian style that depended for its individuality purely on its surface decoration. Tongue and groove boarding in a heavier frame is the normal North American characteristic, with ornamentation of applied turned wood. In Nova Scotia the style is mainly represented by turned ornaments.

It may be most readily remembered as the style of the railways. As an individual style it appears to have its origins in the Gothic Revival, although later it became entangled with Elizabethan or Tudor Revival and then with the Queen Anne Revival.

In Nova Scotian housing it appears mainly in decorative porches, verandahs and gable ends, where the turned wood is used extravagantly, as though the lathes worked overtime and someone had to justify the excess of complex spindles, spools and spokes.

In the gable ends the redundancy reaches its highest level when what is created appears to be more a matter of extravagant bird perches than either structure or sense would demand. Sad to say, this is probably an attempt at humanization when the machines had won the battle over handcraftsmanship. It is not surprising that the Arts and Crafts movement in England tried to put an alternative before the world, but they failed to make their alternative cost-effective. (Compare with Queen Anne Revival p.84)

In Nova Scotia, the Stick style can be very clearly contrasted with its contemporary plain vernacular cousins.

The most noticeable feature is the gable end oversailing the bay, which is then supported by "stick" and "twig" brackets.

Many houses are very close to the Queen Anne Revival in form and elevation and may be hard to distinguish. However, there is often a noticeable stick-work jumble in the top of the gable end or, as in this case, an excessive amount of balustrade.

The stick brackets are obviously not structural. Labour was cheap and the parts were readily available, but the excesses of expression can be compared with the contemporary internal use of lace-fringed antimacassars.

Two examples of pedimented gables give an idea of the style's potential. Sunburst patterns of overlapping wood ornament the lower corners.

In this case, however, a strap design in low relief fills the corners, which is reminiscent of the influence exerted by the English architect George Eastlake, who practised in New York. Both gables rely on a Palladian window as the centrepiece, although both are heavily modified.

The extreme ends to which the style could be taken can be seen in this combination of fretwork and spindle.

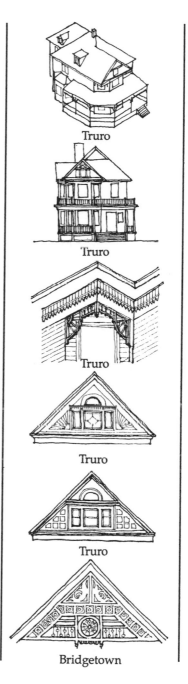

Truro

Truro

Truro

Truro

Truro

Bridgetown

1880-1920

Shingle

The Queen Anne Revival style began by reviving an earlier English tradition as an antidote to the wilder extravagances of the mechanized late-Victorian period. In New England the style was modified by traditional materials and the techniques of coastal building, where some of the best shingle-style houses developed using Queen Anne forms but were simplified to withstand Atlantic gales. Despite the stripping of decoration, the style remained highly romantic, with its random gabling and complex straggling forms.

In the reduction of scale from the expansive summer residences of the very rich in Massachusetts to the more modest houses of Nova Scotia, various changes took place. Following the Low House by McKim, Mead and White in Rhode Island (1887), the style took a radical turn towards simplicity of form, with a lower roof pitch and the elimination of dormer windows or gables.

Both aspects of Shingle style were transported to Nova Scotia, but not in any great number. One remarkable example of each type is extant: the summer home of Alexander Graham Bell near Baddeck (see Vacation); and the Eaton summer house at Deep Cove. But there are many more derivatives of these pure examples, with one particular type needing a style group on its own. This is the Bungalow style of the World War I period. The usual treatment of the shingles is with stain, which is easily discernible; the cladding of porch beams and posts with shingles is more subtle.

Shingle style is not just a matter of the outer covering of the house, but also an integral part of the form, as in these dormer windows.

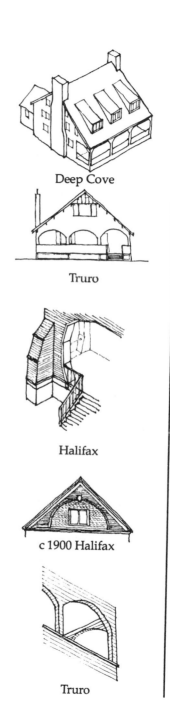

Deep Cove

Here, arches and columns are entirely clad with shingles, as is the balustrade. Elements of Stick and Shingle styles are often combined as they were contemporaries.

Truro

An odd example has a Gothic-style buttress entirely clad in shingles. The curved opening, which is trimmed with straight pieces, is rather surprising. This house was designed by William Harris.

Halifax

Displays of local craft virtuosity take place in the gables. Here an arch is formed out of shingles with a keystone of dubious utility.

c 1900 Halifax

The treatment of arch and column clad on all surfaces with shingles demonstrates the flexibility of the materials and was cheap when wages were low.

Truro

1880-1915
Late Victorian Eclectic

It is very hard to treat the Late-Victorian Eclectic as a serious architectural style. Nevertheless, it must be faced on numerical grounds alone. Many examples exist in Nova Scotia to bear witness to the fruits of civilization. The railways, coastal steamers, and most of all, the mail-service, made information immediately available over vast distances. The newest style variation in the suburbs of New York, Boston or Chicago was read about the next week in Halifax. Complete kits of pressed metal or cast-iron façade were also available by mail order anywhere in North America.

In the same way that the Great Plague was eliminated by the Great Fire of London in 1666, so the "plague" of eclecticism was eliminated by catastrophe—World War I.

Before the war there were cheap materials and labour, combined with a population of extremes of wealth and poverty. After the appalling slaughter of World War I costs rose, and there were too few labourers to allow indulgence in extravaganzas of form and decoration.

These houses became a nightmare to maintain, and many have suffered as rust and rot have diminished their decorative elements. As many of these houses are large, and as the war brought changes to the structure of the household, such as in the number of servants employed, families tended to move to smaller houses. The larger houses were either turned into rooming houses or professional buildings. Many disappeared before World War II, while others became motels, restaurants, funeral homes or small office or professional buildings.

Strangely enough the style was not eliminated. Pick up any current glossy magazine and you will find similar ideas. The eclectic spirit of combining everything in one design still goes marching on.

The key to Eclecticism is complexity, both in stylistic allusions and formal juxtapositions. This tower is not entirely absorbed into the form of the house nor is the style the same, with Italianate form and Gothic Revival details mixed with Stick decorations.

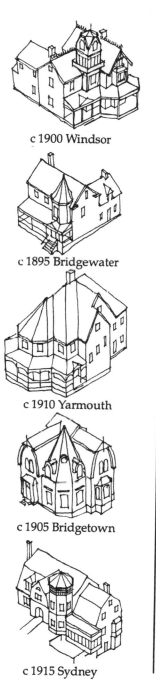

c 1900 Windsor

c 1895 Bridgewater

c 1910 Yarmouth

c 1905 Bridgetown

c 1915 Sydney

The Classic Revival is modified by a French Romanesque Revival tower.

A Stick verandah surrounds a French Romanesque Revival house with little to disclose the style but the stepped windows at the staircase.

As an example of where the lack of rules could lead, the unique curved gambrel roof is combined with a modified French Romanesque tower and Italianate windows. This most extraordinary example is now a precious asset.

The combination of a gambrel roof and tower is not common, but the tower is a reminder of the Shingle style from New England.

1880-1915

Late Victorian Plain

Despite the extravagances of the mid-Victorian era, many houses of simple or straightforward form were built during the same period. The forms varied probably more by regional preference than for stylistic reasons. There were low-pitched or virtually flat roofs, and many roofs were of moderate pitch and hipped.

Among the smaller houses were many that attempted to achieve a country air. There were many with porches that ran parallel to the street, whether on the short or long side of the form. There were simple box forms or more complex T forms. There were bay windows and also some large exposed chimneys, but mostly the chimneys were internal, ending at the ridge.

There seems to be no reason for the simplicity. Maybe it grew out of economic necessity in the smaller houses, but it clearly is used in the large ones as well, although in the largest houses there is discreet decoration around brickwork panels, reminiscent of Sullivan's work in Chicago.

The need for industrial labour forces in undeveloped areas created a need for housing for workmen. Houses built by coal, steel and other companies tended to be plain and in regimented groupings. Decoration was extremely limited.

A single feature can make all the difference between one style and another. Here the roof is flat or nearly flat. The windows are relatively simple, and decoration is minimal but was probably enhanced by painting with different colours.

The low-pitched roof and the verandah evoke an image of rocking chairs and long hot summer days. There is a little of the West in them too!

Even the simplest of doorways were not mean, but were given a little decoration to heighten attention.

The windows show advances in the techniques of glass production by using larger panes. It was not only the factory that mattered but also improvements in transportation.

Steeper pitched roofs were also common and often matched the roof pitch of the verandah. This form was popular in areas of rapid growth, or as housing for industry.

Extravagance was limited to certain parts of the house such as this stained glass window. Sometimes rather crude, these windows often used primary colours around the central pane of plain or textured glass. The corner squares are often coloured red and blue.

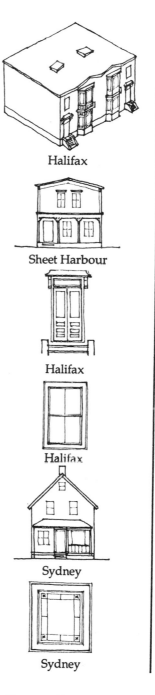

Halifax

Sheet Harbour

Halifax

Halifax

Sydney

Sydney

Any Period

Transitions

Purely for reasons of economy in this book, the buildings that fit into more than one style category are brought together. They are an interesting bunch and show signs of influence unlike any other category.

In some cases the style is a hybrid of two consecutive styles caught in the act of changing. In other cases it is an earlier style with later additional parts that may or may not be of a consecutive style. In cases where a plurality of styles appears to have been intended from the start, it is given a name all on its own—Late Victorian Eclectic—which is an expression of a particularly extravagant period of extremes, especially in fashion and furniture.

In the typical transition where a new style is appearing out of an older one, there are both gentle and sensitive amalgams, such as Ionic columns at the porch with a Gothic window overhead.

In some cases, for example where a later alteration introduced a dormer window of a different style from the original house, aspects of good design, such as scale, tend to be ignored for the sake of utility. Some alterations are simply brutal surgery with no sensitivity at all, such as when two different buildings are joined together while the window sills are left at different heights and with window sashes of different types.

In some cases there are delightful and subtle shocks; in others, a crude jarring of sensibilities.

The need for energy efficiency is causing a radical change to the housing stock of Nova Scotia, often with little sensitivity. The most recent transition style must be the "early improvement to more energy efficient" transition, with storm windows and prefinished siding. Sometimes windows are blocked up and brick chimneys removed.

Elegant Ionic columns supporting the porch roof do not seem to mind the Gothic windows above them, but the integrity of the Greek is far better than the Gothic in this example. The bargeboards have too large a pattern.

This Gothic-shaped house has no trim and appears never to have had any. The shape of gable with its steep pitch suggests that it is late.

From the front this house is a late Italianate/French Second Empire house, but from the side is Gothic Revival. The rear wing is pure Second Empire. This may have been built at one time, which would make it more properly Eclectic.

This large cottage has Stick gable trim and a Gothic bay window. The windows have Gothic-like trim as hood mouldings, and the bargeboards are of a Stick type, known as Eastlake in the United States.

This is a Classic Revival house with an extension on which is a Gothic-shaped cross gable.

This typical Gothic Revival form has been given Italianate windows throughout.

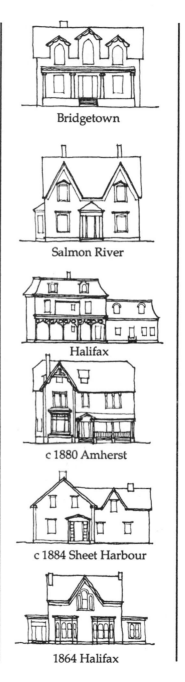

Bridgetown

Salmon River

Halifax

c 1880 Amherst

c 1884 Sheet Harbour

1864 Halifax

1880-1915

Chateauesque
This style for larger houses is very similar to Eclectic but differs from it in one precise and fundamental way. In Eclecticism everything is put into one building; in Chateauesque each building is true to one style. There were many styles to choose from, and several variants can be seen in Nova Scotia.

Scottish Neo-Baronial was popular in areas where stone was available, but it needed manicured lawns and rhododendrons to set it off. It was essentially a countryhouse style.

Baroque Revival was suitable for more urban sites and probably was chosen because the owner had more conservative taste.

Neo-Georgian was ideally built in brick or dressed stone and would have been suitable for a bank manager, as his new bank was very likely to be in a similar style.

Castle style was for those aspiring to the Senate or philanthropy. It tended towards grandeur and other tycoon attributes. Naturally there would be a need for sources of the true style. These were available in books, some of which are extravagant in their colour printing and quality of reproduction. But by now there were architectural magazines eager to publish the work of architects who specialized in revival styles. Many architects in the business of restoring the originals were able to reproduce authentic details.

Unlike the Eclectic designs, these houses had an air of fidelity to the original models which, in some cases, is quite uncanny, especially when craftsmanship and materials were of a high quality. Unfortunately they are relatively rare in Nova Scotia.

This has a true castle quality with elegant late-Victorian conservatory, crenelated chimneys and Scottish gable ends. "Scottish Baronial" is a style that was popular in Europe, but there are few examples in Nova Scotia.

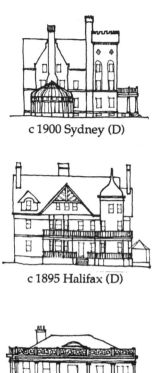

c 1900 Sydney (D)

The combination of sheer size in a landscaped setting is made even more impressive by the use of the tower and, especially, the double-layer verandah. The general effect is of Queen Anne Revival style, despite the balconies and onion dome on the tower.

c 1895 Halifax (D)

A relatively sensitive example of the Classic Revival, with small pilasters and quite extravagant balustrade. The balustrade is used to add pattern and also to raise the profile of the house and make it appear larger. This Southern plantation type of house appears out of place in Nova Scotia.

1906 Hubbards

1900-1930

Cottage

Around the period of World War I many different influences impinged on the housing of Nova Scotia. The revolution that took place in the trenches of Europe had its visible effect in the post-war houses.

One of the shocking results of the Great War was the destruction of one out of every eight men in Canada who were eligible for military service. This in turn resulted in the elevation of labourers to soldiers, putting them on the bottom rung of a social ladder that implied greater social status, even to the point of owning property.

During the post-war years increased wages, improved health standards and space provisions generated a change in the demand for housing. This new housing was unlike the compact urban dwellings in large cities. The houses, though small, were detached and reminiscent of the English cottage.

One influence was the result of research that had been carried out on ethnic origins. Books were being published on early architecture, and a new pride was taken in the roots of one's family. This seems to have been particularly true of the Dutch who became proud of their roots after Teddy Roosevelt became President in 1901. There was a sudden upsurge in gambrel roofs, swept eaves and large dormers.

Another specific influence at this time was the devastation caused by the Halifax Explosion. The demand for replacement housing was complicated by the need to rebuild the strategic port. Fortunately, the military need provided enough support to encourage immediate reconstruction. In terms of architecture there were expedient solutions, and much of the housing was therefore plain. The main example of housing built from relief funding is dealt with separately under Hydrostone, but the larger quantity of independent houses largely fits into the category of cottage. The north end of Halifax, which took up to 20 years to rebuild after 1917, has many such examples.

Several different forms of cottage were developed. Possibly the most easily seen is the one with a truncated or hipped gable. The verandah or porch, facing the street, becomes a social point during the summer months.

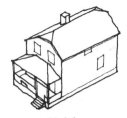

Halifax

The Dutch influence became popular after a surge of interest in ethnic origins caused many people in the United States to build replicas in the Dutch style. Typical features are the large dormer windows in the gambrel roof, eyebrow windows and the change of roof pitch to form a skirt. The eyebrow windows are the least authentic detail.

Halifax

The simplicity of the hipped roof on this cottage is in direct contrast with the abundant decoration and general extravagance of the immediately preceding styles. The extreme economy is all the more poignant as this example was built following the Halifax Explosion and World War I.

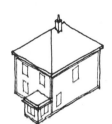

Halifax

1910-1940

Bungalow

Small family houses in the expanding suburbs during the 1920s were quite often built in the Bungalow style. The title initially refers more to form than to style. During this period certain elements were included that created a distinctive appearance and also provided opportunity for development. The roof is typically low-pitched with large overhangs and exposed rafter ends. The houses are two-storeyed, usually pretending to be single-storeyed.

It seems likely that the Bungalow style grew out of the earlier Shingle style, as there are examples of stained shingles in both styles. However, one remarkable and distinctive feature separates them: a short but distorted column holding up the porch makes some look as though they have suffered an overload and swelled too much at the bottom; others are of distorted proportion without precedent in architecture. The effect is further exaggerated by the column being placed on top of a shingled balustrade or parapet wall, which is sometimes excessively tapered. The column is often square, but variations include circular, paired and inverted. Within the general style, a substyle called Chalet developed. This stretched the form to generate more protection for a full-width gable end verandah and also provided opportunity for some shingle decoration with an Alpine twist.

Bungalow style continued to be built until World War II, but degenerated in the scale and quality of its exposed structural members. It appears to have been more popular in the rest of Canada than in Nova Scotia.

Most recognizable is the large roof that sweeps down to form the front porch. It is also usual to find a large dormer window that in other parts of Canada was used as a sleeping porch.

In elevation the most noticeable detail is the porch column. All the classical rules of proportion are broken for a column of exaggerated shape.

Doors are rather plain, often with glazing. The porch is designed as the entry; the door is secondary to it.

There are a number of odd details that keep reappearing, one of which is the expression of structure, even to the shaping of beams. This is a direct influence from the Arts and Crafts movement in Britain or from the Swiss Chalet.

Sometimes eaves are supported on large brackets and often the shingles are given a new texture by alternating wide and narrow courses.

It is in the short column that the style is most daring and original, with all sorts of variations, many of them without precedent. The column sits on the porch hand-rail and can be solid and shingled, or a regular balustrade. Single columns are often square in cross section and excessively tapered.

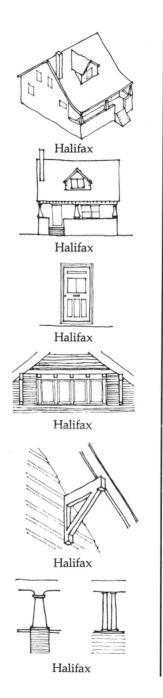

Halifax

Halifax

Halifax

Halifax

Halifax

Halifax

1919
Hydrostone

Hydrostone is a type-variation that was part of the rebuilding programme following the 1917 Halifax Explosion, when housing was required quickly and in large quantity. In an area to the west of Fort Needham, an estate was planned very similar in layout to those used in the English garden suburbs a few years earlier. Designed by an English architect in Montreal for the Halifax Relief Commission, the housing retains its foreign atmosphere to this day. The green open spaces in front and the narrow lanes behind the row houses have only recently begun to be copied in condominium developments. But in the Hydrostone area, there are private gardens and garages behind.

The word Hydrostone comes from the tradename of a particular hollow concrete block made in a special factory at Eastern Passage. Not all the houses in the area now generally called the Hydrostone actually used the block. Unfortunately, the concrete block has a low thermal resistance, thus many of the houses are currently being altered as different types of siding and a little thermal insulation are applied. Because of the individual ownership there is little coordination of effort, and some very strange mixtures of textures can now be seen that partially destroy the calm unity and subtle variation within the original scheme.

The choice of the style is in direct contrast with the material from which it was constructed. Whereas the English garden suburbs were all designed in the Arts and Crafts tradition, which implied Queen Anne Revival style, Tudor Revival style or a general English Cottage style, the Hydrostone houses are not of brick and tile, but of concrete and stucco made to look like wood and plaster.

The layout is as important as the individual houses or terraces. This stems from the very popular current designs of the English garden suburb. Of note is the divided access, public and private, and the individual gardens, which compare favourably with modern condominiums.

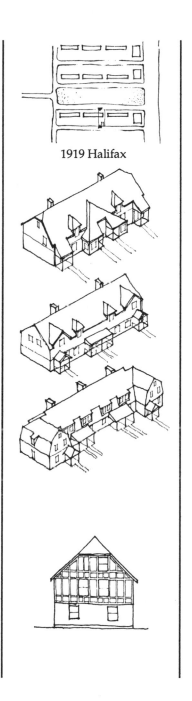

1919 Halifax

The string of cottages can be seen in several different forms, and of special note is the way that variety is introduced, despite many similar plan arrangements. Modern designers are beginning to look back and see the advantages of this simplicity with variety.

In all cases the front porch is seen as an important place for social interaction. It is here that British Socialism is at its most persuasive in housing, providing a quality of life within a restricted budget.

There are some curiosities when the scale is reduced. The upper level is often rendered over and moulded to appear like Tudor half-timbering.

Modern Architecture

One event of major architectural significance in the twentieth century took place in Europe after 1910. This was the development of the style known as Modern or, more recently, as the International style. "International" implies that the style caught on and spread beyond Europe. This was the first totally original architectural style to be developed in about 200 years. There are no true examples among Nova Scotia houses, but the style is included because elsewhere it was very influential. Through secondary influences, features such as the picture window entered the architecture of this time.

Modern architecture, the modern movement, functionalism or the International style, as this style has been called at different times, is rare in Nova Scotia for a number of reasons. Perhaps the most important reason has been its apparent irrelevance to the housing needs of the population. It only became an influence after it had been well-diluted in other regions of North America. White concrete walls with horizontal strip windows, plain surfaced panels of bright primary colours, industrial materials, plate glass windows with metal frames, glass block walls and most noticeably flat roofs—these were the hallmarks. Rather more dramatically the interiors were filled with chromeplated metal tube furniture often upholstered in fine leather or even white fur. This was a far cry from the Nova Scotia of rocking chairs and the remnants of the Queen Anne Revival.

Berlin and Paris were the centres of the style's development before World War I and, after the war, examples could be found from Barcelona to Moscow. Architects such as Walter Gropius and Mies van der Rohe in Germany and le Corbusier in France led the movement and continued to amaze their followers, even to the ends of their long lives, with their design virtuosity.

After World War I many Nova Scotians moved south to look for work. The depleted population of Nova Scotia had no need of this alien style that was based on industrialization, new ideas about form and space, the use of materials and new patterns of urban development. Open plans with perimeter walls of only glass and metal, flat roofs and machine precision were simply incompatible with the climate and the ideas of comfort for Nova Scotians. In Europe, where the style originated, the rich and intelligentsia indulged themselves. In England, the style was never accepted as there was no indigenous architect of international stature. When Adolf Hitler forced many of the major architects to flee to other countries, they chose to leave Europe altogether and travelled to the United States where the style flourished even during World War II. It is probably too soon to assess the true value of the style, but the pure expression found its origins in about 1910 in Austria and Germany, and one critic even suggests that it ended in 1931 with the Barcelona Pavilion. Many of the buildings associated with the style were built after World War II, and it was at this time that a modest influence was registered in Nova Scotia, resulting in a limited use of large plain glass window, flush door, flat roof, materials such as brick arranged in bands or panels. The remnants of the style can be seen in the tube steel posts holding up front door canopies and in the pipe handrails that were typically used in the originals.

It is easier to find houses in Nova Scotia whose style betrays a reaction against modern architecture than ones whose style is clearly derived from it. Pitched roofs, small windows, shingled walls and a lack of white paint are the long-lasting tradition of Nova Scotia and look as though they will remain so for a long time to come.

It appears that the end of the twentieth century may well end as it began, in a flurry of decoration and bright colour, to which another generation will react. This style is related to Modern only as the basis from which to deviate. It is called Post Modern.

1930-1940

Art Moderne

Art moderne, moderne, modernistic and art deco are all the same movement really, though some of the details provide a different thrust. As a style it developed on both sides of the Atlantic but went further in North America. The influence of the movies and the automobile caused it to become a flashy style in some examples, such as the Rockefeller Center in New York City, and therefore it rapidly became dated.

The term "art deco" suggests decoration; indeed, the style seems to have been generated in reaction to the purity of modern architecture in Europe. Although the two are from the same root they are remarkably different, one without decoration and the other with it. Perhaps the most enduring examples of the style are the gas stations and furniture of the period.

In the houses of Nova Scotia the most readily recognizable elements are the flat roof to wall connection with no overhang, the use of corner windows with a strong horizontal emphasis in the glazing bars and the sometimes indiscriminate use of circular windows. Vertical strips of glass block are often incorporated to light the staircases. Some examples of stucco can be found and even some rounded corners in the walls, but the style was more usually adapted to the indigenous materials of Nova Scotia, either shingle or brick, neither of which is readily translated into curved walls of small radius.

To many people the style of Art Moderne is epitomized in the New York skyscraper. The problems of reducing the scale from skyscraper to house and of building the style in Nova Scotia seem insurmountable. Of all the details the corner window must be the most telling, as an essentially framed timber wall attempts to copy a diaphragm wall and ends up with a hefty post right in the corner to block the view and destroy the argument for spatial freedom.

A flat roof, complex forms and corner windows are typical. Protective roofs over doors are often rounded or, if placed in an angle, are given a quarter round. A tall corner window usually denotes the stair.

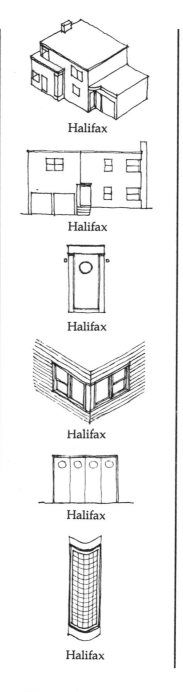

Halifax

The form may be derived from massing of space requirements, but the elevation is an early demonstration of response to the site.

Halifax

A circular window set in a front door becomes a common feature. The Classical details stripped of decoration are also common.

Halifax

Corner windows are used regardless of the function. The whole effect from inside is largely compromised by the structural necessity of a corner post in the wood frame construction. The European original would have been made of reinforced concrete and steel sash with no interruption of the glass.

Halifax

Garage doors pick up the circular window motif.

Halifax

By far the most easily recognized detail is the tall staircase window with its translucent glass blocks, which were manufactured for flat walls or for rounded corners.

Halifax

1940-1945

World War II Prefabricated

In centres of industrial activity, where migrant workers had to be housed in a hurry, areas of prefabricated housing were built at astonishing rates during World War II. To achieve a high volume of production with economy, the houses were built on post foundations and to a very limited set of design variables. Inevitably, economy also meant a restriction in size.

At the same time that the wartime economy forced limitations on the internal accommodation, it also restricted decoration on the outside. The original designs were actually superb models of efficient lowcost housing. A major criticism of these projects is the site layout, where the rows of small houses are lined up with little consideration of privacy or individuality, devoid of planting. In the context in which they were built we have to remember that they were designed with a limited life expectancy. Groups can be found in places such as Amherst, Halifax, New Glasgow and Pictou. Their longevity remains as a tribute to their original designers and builders and to their ability to sustain changes.

Where these houses can be seen today they tend to have been placed on concrete foundation walls, and although many remain small, some have been extended both horizontally and vertically. Some have even been lifted and a new storey added at ground level. Some have had their roofs removed and different roofshapes built on, such as a Mansard.

The basic house is compact but relatively high out of the ground. It is quite usual for these houses to have been built on post foundations and to have had basements built under them later.

Halifax

The window patterns suggest the internal arrangements of rooms, with only a limited range of layouts. Economy of materials in the wartime period is seen in the modest overhang, decoration, and in the small overall size.

Halifax

Doors are plain and simple and yet are dated by being panelled rather than flush.

Halifax

Windows are small but, rather surprisingly, are not too simple, and are formed out of small panes.

Halifax

Porches are often added later as one means of personal expression. They may be unprotected platforms or roofed shelters of various sizes that offer some protection from the weather. The illustration shows steps for a house on a steep slope.

Halifax

1940-1960
American Modern

The pedigree of American Modern is quite distinctly different from either Modern, Art Moderne or Art Deco. The inspiration for American Modern came from houses designed by Frank Lloyd Wright. In the 1930s and 1940s, he designed a number of modest houses that he called Usonian, for citizens of the United States. The influence on domestic architecture was considerable, in both the United States and Canada. A universal attempt was made to recreate the strong horizontal emphasis and suburban character of the originals, often without enough site width, usually because Wright's planning intentions had not been understood. The original Usonian houses employed flat roofs at several different levels, boarded fascias on overhanging eaves, brick walls with a large brick chimney and large areas of glass facing the sun. Wright shunned the use of basements, but most of the derivatives incorporate basements.

Some of the copies used shingles instead of brickwork or clapboard and yet all seem to copy one element of the original. This was an edge to the roof that consisted not of one piece of wood, but of three pieces, each superimposed outside of the one below to give an effect of outward tilt to the fascia. The extreme overhang was meant to emphasize the horizontal. In his Rosenbaum House, Frank Lloyd Wright cantilevered the carport roof more than 18 feet, more suitable to Alabama's rain than Nova Scotia's snow.

Flat roofs are difficult to maintain in Nova Scotia. There may be some connection between the technical difficulties and the relatively small number of examples. The American Modern style was short-lived and made a negligible influence on the exterior appearance of houses, but internally, the open plan that was fundamental to the design was incorporated into all succeeding designs.

Flat roofs, and wide overhangs and multiple planes are typical identifying parts of the form. A split level section is also common.

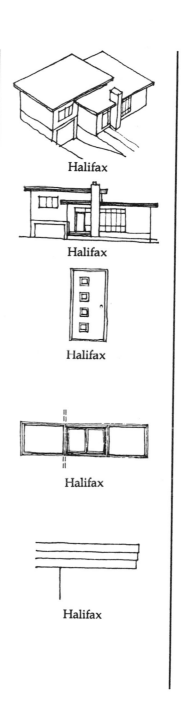

Halifax

A carefully balanced geometric pattern has prominent chimneys and extensive glazing. Wright's influence can be seen in the different flat roof planes.

Halifax

Asymmetric decoration has been used in very small areas. On the whole, little decoration is used; rather, the materials are normally left natural.

Halifax

Small windows are often gathered together to form strips of glazing, lighting more than one room behind the face. From outside it is almost impossible to tell where the interior walls are located.

Halifax

An easily distinguishable feature is the flat roof and wide overhang, which is often finished with three overlapping square-edged boards.

Halifax

1940+

New England Revival

During the 1940s houses started to appear that were indiscernible from those built 200 years before. There was a return to the simple house forms brought here by the first settlers from New England. These were mostly of one-and-half-storeys, and one architect in particular was highly influential in Nova Scotia, Andrew Cobb.

Typically the houses were called Cape Cod, though most builders rejected the austerity of the real thing and rather favoured the well-developed moulded façade treatment of this ubiquitous house form. As a form it can be found anywhere from Labrador to Virginia, but mostly in the states of Maine, Massachusetts, Rhode Island and Connecticut. Having achieved an acceptance as an historic design, the replicas suffered from one major problem, that of enlargement. Unfortunately, the many early solutions could not be copied as modern urban sites were smaller and plumbing inhibited certain options. To incorporate bathrooms large dormers were included at construction, thus a number of these houses look rather different from the back compared with the front.

The typical Nova Scotian house goes back to the 1750 or 1775 models used in this province and Nova Scotians have built storey-and-a-half houses, often with small dormer windows or else two-storey houses with straight walls.

For the casual inquirer, the easiest way to discern the original from the copy is to look at the top of the roof where most older houses have a sagging ridge. At ground level the foundation wall would have been of stone or brick but nowadays is more likely to be poured concrete, unless a careful reproduction has been built. Although the style might be named Nova Scotia Revival, it seems that the most recent design sources used are largely from the United States rather than from Nova Scotia.

The rear roof slope is modified to allow an upstairs bathroom, which suggests that the form is incorrect for its purpose. Chimneys are often smaller than the eighteenth century originals.

Halifax

Replicas can usually be spotted by the oversized dormer windows, quite possibly due to building code requirements for more glass and higher ceilings. A lack of chimney may also indicate electric heating.

Halifax

Doors are sometimes elaborately correct, even to copies of period door hardware and knocker. The effect is immediately nullified by the fake carriage lamps on either side, obviously twentieth century electric light fixtures.

Halifax

Vertical sliding sash windows are common, with wooden glazing bars that are noticeably thicker than the originals. Shutters are also normally present, though anachronistic and nonfunctional. On closer inspection it may be found that storm windows or double glazing or snap out plastic glazing bars may date the window as recent.

Halifax

1945-1960

Contemporary

Following the baby boom after World War II and the subsequent consumer boom, there was in due time a building boom, which had a dramatic influence on the fringes of many communities in Nova Scotia.

Some curious things happened. A design developed for sloping sites, the split level, became a universal craze. Thanks to the bulldozer, this design could be used on any site. The straggling Ranch style from California was also universally lauded, regardless of heat losses from its extensive perimeter and large areas of glass. The new rationalized technology of post-and-beam construction used on the west coast became another universally accepted type of design. The advent of a car for everyone encouraged the use of the carport, which could be filled in as extra living space when the family grew in size.

Generally the designs used brick and artificial stone veneer with lots of glass and low-pitched roofs. In some cases there are lowpitched roofs using asphalt shingles and in others nearly flat roofs with tar and gravel finish, often at two levels and sometimes pitching in towards the middle. Strips of windows sometimes alternate actual windows with fixed panels.

Use of materials was carefully considered, and natural materials and finishes became important. "Honesty" became the buzzword of the period, but little difference can be discerned between the houses of twenty years before or after this particular style.

The inward sloping roofs defy the Nova Scotia climate, while the stepped roofs respond to the split-level design.

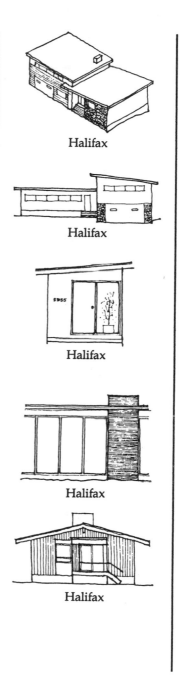

Halifax

The low-pitched roof planes may slope in more than one direction. Horizontal lines are emphasized by the change in surface material. The slogan "honesty of expression" ensured materials could be seen in their natural state.

Halifax

Solid doors are juxtaposed with sheet glass windows, which then had to be filled with plants to avoid ambiguity. Mistaking a window of fixed glass for an open door is dangerous.

Halifax

Elements of the form are arranged to interpenetrate, as the chimney passes through the roof plane and also forms part of the wall, while simultaneously dividing the spaces inside.

Halifax

A much publicized modular building technique developed in New England by Carl Koch has had a far-reaching effect, even into Nova Scotia. White painted trim contrasts with vertical redwood siding. This is very different from the above examples but fits into the general style.

Halifax

1950+

Government Assisted

For most of this century the Federal Government has been involved in promoting better housing. Standards of sanitation, storage, ventilation, food preparation, noise separation, fire safety, durability and comfort have each been tackled, and with the introduction of the first National Building Code in 1941, a universal Canadian standard came into force. Whether through free pamphlets produced for the Department of Health in the 1920s or free books of designs provided by the Central Mortgage and Housing Corporation in the 1960s, the result has been a centrally controlled uniformity of standards and designs applied indiscriminately across the country. It is quite reasonable to assume common space standards for a four-person family anywhere in Canada, but it is unreasonable to presume that the houses should look alike across the whole country.

One thing is quite certain, the National Housing Act has benefited many Canadians. In some other countries, cheaper housing is plagued by all the problems that result when too many people are squeezed into too small a space. In Canada, because of the standards promoted by the National Housing Act, this has often not been the case. Over the past fifty years, as a result of both direct and indirect government support, there has been a continual investment in public and private housing in this country, and this has produced some houses of high quality, both inside and out.

The military and other services have also required housing, causing the federal government to be a developer on a grand scale. Housing for military personnel has tended towards a universal solution produced from a centralized office. Whether houses or low-rise, high-density apartments, the appearance is towards uniformity, encouraged by the same colour paint, lack of individuality in planting and the isolation caused by extensive chain-link fences.

The bungalow is in many ways the characteristic contemporary Canadian house,
but it is sometimes built with a change in
surface decoration which also lends it a
degree of regionalism.

Dartmouth

The split level, which is ideally suited to
a sloping site, is very seldom built on one.
Even when a site has contoured land, the
developer often flattens it to fit in more
houses, and in the process even removes
mature trees to avoid the increase in costs
associated with adjusting the design and
building between them.

Hants Co.

The split entry, with many style variations and material options on the exterior,
is essentially no different from the bungalow in its use of space.

Forest Hills

Co-ops often provide well-designed, affordable homes for people of lower in-
comes. In this example of Halifax County
co-operative housing, the design is certainly equal to what you might expect
from housing financed in more traditional ways. It is interesting to compare this
with Halifax's Hydrostone housing,
which in some ways it resembles.

Forest Hills

1970+

Prefabricated

As a result of a continuing need for cheaper housing, prefabrication emerged as one solution. There are two main types: complete offsite construction or onsite assembly of a kit of pre-manufactured parts, either precut pieces or larger prefabricated elements.

The complete offsite prefabrication is limited to single-storey houses usually split down the ridge and often having eaves that are hinged to reduce the width taken up on the highway. The halves are put together on a prepared foundation, and in just a few hours the sewer, water and power connections are completed and the furniture moved in. Naturally the shapes are limited to what is most easy to tow!

Precut and partially prefabricated houses vary from ones that simply supply all the pieces in the right sizes and quantities to ones that offer pre-assembled wall, floor and roof units. Prefabrication inhibits owners from making late changes in the design, but construction and assembly can be very fast.

Since there is no stigma attached to owning a prefabricated car, the attitude toward owning a prefabricated house seems just a bit odd. But it is virtually impossible to identify a house built from precut components; when such a house is finished it appears no different from one built conventionally.

With prefabrication the quality of manufacturing can be guaranteed because the house is built inside a factory and, with supervision always at hand, the result can be high quality work, quickly done, with economic use of materials. As the standard of building is required to be higher in the latest energy-efficient houses, we may see more use of prefabrication to achieve faultless vapour barriers, for example. Because there is no influence of weather on the sequence of building, normally difficult processes, such as insulation inside a roof space, can be done before the outer surfaces are installed.

When a house is bought as a kit, the contractor merely assembles the parts and the result may look very traditional. The less prefabricaton there is, the more opportunity the owner has for last-minute design changes and personal treatments.

Even quite large houses can be purchased in kit form. Part of the cost-saving is in onsite erection time and the lack of waste.

Partially prefabricated as a set of components, the panelled house can be rapidly assembled, with fine tolerances allowing for great accuracy. The number of parts may be limited to keep costs manageable.

Factory built in two halves, these houses can be installed in one day. Interior layouts may vary widely, but outside they vary little, except in finish details such as the windows, for example.

Looking most like a mobile home, the recent smallest prefab arrives on-site as a complete finished building, only needing a foundation and services.

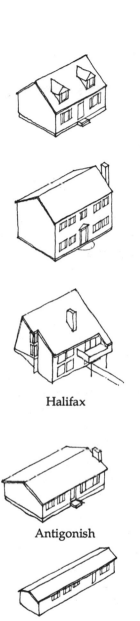

Halifax

Antigonish

1950+

Apartment/ Condominium

The style is invariably chosen as a part of an image to be sold. Names are part of the sales strategy as well; for example, words such as "court", "lane" and "terrace" conjure up architectural images that are seldom realized.

It is important to remember that style has implications for society but that it is also generated by society, or at least by an elite group within society. Often style seems to have been "just provided" and a variety of constraints seem to forbid its alteration. Style gets associated with development policy and then manages to limit the shape of our new landscapes.

For example, it is generally believed that in an apartment building of six or more floors there is little to be done but to accept the nature of layered dwellings with balconies. Such buildings in Nova Scotia are most often no different from those found in Toronto and may in fact have been designed there. But high-density, low or medium-rise schemes can be found that do not inevitably turn out to be slabs or towers, and which provide far better amenities and offer less shock to the surrounding houses.

In general, apartment buildings in Nova Scotia are small, plain boxes which are close to being without style.

A surprisingly large percentage of the population of Nova Scotia—17 per cent—lives in apartments and condominiums.

As a separate type of dwelling, condominiums cannot be discerned from the exterior unless they are of the house type. Early condominium developments were of the townhouse form, and recently built expensive developments have used this same form. You may recognize the type through its central door, canopy or porte cochere, or from the lack of individual yards.

Really tall Apartment/Condominiums are still quite scarce in Nova Scotia, and they are not illustrated.

Financial returns tend to dominate architectural opportunities in this form and generate a minimal building with perhaps some dressing up at the front. A squat box is cheapest.

The elevation clearly suggests the spine corridor on each floor.

Doors are usually of aluminum with sidelights. Sometimes the handle is customized, but is more often just an aluminum push bar designed to withstand furniture removals.

Windows are often horizontal sliders, the early ones having a lot of air leakage.

While entry doors and windows in general suggest that everything is bought "off the shelf," some buildings display remarkable virtuosity in entrance canopies.

The corners provide the clearest statement of the attitude to decoration. The front face is given a cosmetic veneer of brick, with sides of vinyl clapboard. Later schemes exhibit more integrity and, in some cases, considerable expense.

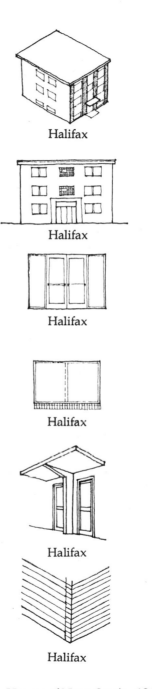

Halifax

Halifax

Halifax

Halifax

Halifax

Halifax

1970+

Log

Few early log houses exist, or at least few have logs that are still visible. Following the California "flower power" period during the 1960s, there was a resurgent interest in "older ways" and in doing all sorts of things, from making cheese from one's own goats' milk to going through the ritual of buying land, settling it and living off it. The ultimate product of back-to-the-land technology was the Log house, especially if the logs were cut on the site.

Modern research has shown that the Log house has certain advantages in energy consumption during the construction stage, especially if hand tools are used and no truck is employed to bring the lumber to the site. When finished, however, the natural Log house provides very poor insulation value unless insulated with a separate wall system inside. In addition, the joints between the logs need an annual inspection for airtightness and freedom from rot.

A newer form of solid wood walling, using milled lumber that fits together with double tongues and grooves, provides a windproof construction but still has a poor thermal resistance value unless separately insulated.

Whether rough or milled lumber is used, the form of construction is very obvious with the crossed corners. Both types suffer from the same potential weakness, which is in the exposed end grain of the lumber. Unless properly protected, this distinguishing stylistic feature is also a potential Achilles' heel. Typically, the low pitched roofs extend well beyond the walls to protect the joints.

In the past, log buildings in Nova Scotia were clad externally with shingles for better weather protection and were typically given a second internal plaster wall for better control of wind infiltration. The modern examples that expose the logs both inside and out demand a great deal of the wood itself, which has to contend with radically different climates inside and out.

Roof pitch is normally low and the form simple rather than complex. The projecting corners are very obvious and are easily seen at a distance as a distinguishing feature.

Use of round logs for rafters generates a strong pattern at the eaves, and the discipline of the construction material influences the position and shape of openings for doors and windows.

The style of door will vary according to age and the shape of the logs being used.

The extreme contrast between the rough wall and the precision of the window and glass is often left without a transition. To avoid weakening the wall too much, the jambs may be faced with a strong board.

Three main types of log construction are used in Canada: round and rough, machined and precise, or cord, otherwise called stackwall. Each is seen clearly at the corners. Stackwall is not at all common in Nova Scotia, probably as it exposes even more end grain to the weather, thus increasing the possibility of rot and leaking.

Details are typically rustic in the house of round logs and more refined in the machined ones. The quality of the whole is most easily determined from inside.

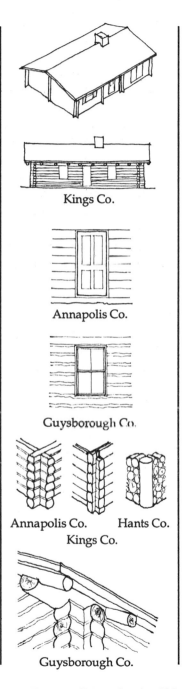

Kings Co.

Annapolis Co.

Guysborough Co.

Annapolis Co.   Hants Co.
Kings Co.

Guysborough Co.

1973+

Ecology

In response to the energy crisis of the 1970s, several alternative ways of building houses have been tried in Nova Scotia. Some energy-saving modifications have been made that have dramatically changed the appearance of houses, the most notable among them being the use of externally applied insulation. On the other hand, woodstove and heatpump installations have been almost invisible. A few prefabricated metal chimney tops do not destroy an architectural style. But neither modification of the skin nor modification of the working parts can constitute a style of itself.

Far more influential on style are the solar, greenhouse and underground house types. All rely on a geometrical relationship to the sun and, for their efficiency, on glass or collectors facing the sun with only small areas of glass elsewhere.

Less obvious, but perhaps the only truly economically sensible alternative, is the super-insulated house, which may be recognised by its deeply inset windows and overall lack of glass except on the south side. In this group the heat loss through the fabric of the house is minimized. Economically the least expensive, it is also stylistically the least obtrusive.

Here history is repeating itself. The Acadians not only sited their houses with the long side facing south, but they also chose south-facing slopes, used trees and barns for windbreaks, and had few openings on the north. Typically the main door and windows were built on the south, with perhaps another door to the east or west. We learn slowly!

Well-insulated houses may not appear to be radically different from any others, except in their windows, which mainly face the south. The brick chimney suggests a moderate view towards energy efficiency.

Lack of a chimney may indicate a super-insulated house, with very low heat loss. Maximizing solar gain may encourage building the house into a bank or making the north walls low.

Solar collection is through panels, which are difficult to hide and may be placed on the roof or low at the edge of a deck where they do not show so much but are more susceptible to shading.

The solar greenhouse may be used as a lobby to the house by creating an intermediate buffer zone that can accept wider variations of temperature than living spaces. It is also possible to sit in the winter sun in one's own jungle.

The underground house achieves greater heat retention through the thermal insulation of the earth, except when it is wet.

Active solar systems impose special constraints on the designer, particularly since the angles of orientation and tilt of the collector are so critical to its maximum efficiency.

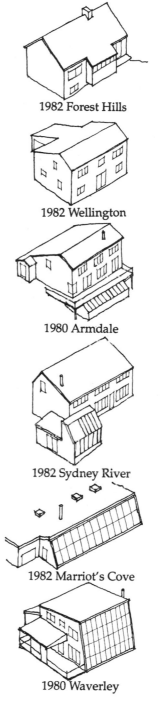

1982 Forest Hills

1982 Wellington

1980 Armdale

1982 Sydney River

1982 Marriot's Cove

1980 Waverley

Houses of Nova Scotia 125

1940+
Revivalist

Among the most recent revivals have been those based on historical models. There is a growing trend towards a style of historicism in which old styles can be used but with modern materials and conveniences. The New England Colonial cupola with weathervane now vents the air conditioner. There are antique lamps modelled on gas street lamp designs from the 1850s but triggered by remote switches sensitive to the amount of daylight. There are doors for the coach house, but the proportion has been changed from vertical to horizontal and the power-operated doors are radio-controlled from within the car. Statuary and Classical Corinthian columns can be found in glass-reinforced plastics, so the whole can be both accurate in detail and much more resistant to frost or rot than either stone or painted wood.

It is curious that in the space age, revivals are thought to be necessary. Perhaps seeking after a bygone elegance is more a cry for something to stay still just for a while, than any real pretention or attempt at self-aggrandizement.

Unfortunately, most 1970s Revivalist houses appear to be from designs built in the United States rather than from Canadian designs. It is conceivable that the owners brought their designs with them but more likely that they purchased drawings that arrived by mail. Perhaps the growing number of these houses demonstrates the lack of a common basis for choosing a house design and the failure of designers to meet the public need. Perhaps developers are striving for originality, or society still sees the only hope for comfortable, cosy housing in styles of the past, not of the present.

English Tudor Revival from the 1920s was popular during the period following World War II and is still being built.

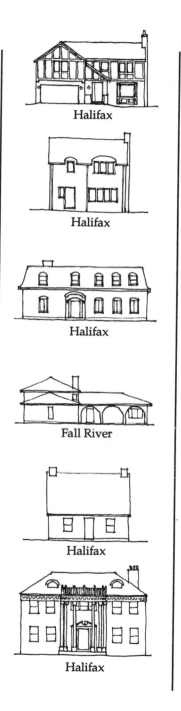

Halifax

Another style copied for its cosy appearance was the English Cottage. There are reminders of thatch roofing in the roof/window treatment.

Halifax

French in detail but not in shape, this horizontal house has curved tops to the brick openings, the dormer windows and the porch, but lacks the mouldings and thicknesses to be really effective.

Halifax

It is surprising to find that there are even Spanish influences in the province, but these are almost all in the form of porches or arcades, which provide shelter from snow rather than from sun.

Fall River

New England shapes recur, although many are changed into Nova Scotian ones by the subtle moving of chimneys, no doubt unconsciously.

Halifax

Influence from the Deep South appears to be new and may stem from television programmes. The example is a greatly simplified version of the Governor's Mansion at Jackson, Mississippi, 1841.

Halifax

1960+

Nova Scotia Vernacular Revival

Many theories have been formulated to show that a region's architecture is related to the culture of the region, the building materials available, the climate and a variety of social influences. Permanent native housing, similar to the Huron longhouse, does not appear to have existed in Nova Scotia prior to settlement by the French. So what is unique to Nova Scotia? What is valuable and enjoyable enough to replicate—at least in spirit, if not in detail—in the housing of today? This question has taxed academics, as well as architects, developers and many homeowners. It seems to be generally accepted that a true Nova Scotian house is not easy to find, and nowhere is it clearly stated just what might constitute such a house. The province appears to be more readily recognized for its natural features than for its manmade ones.

If this book proves anything, it must be that the range of styles in use in Nova Scotia over nearly four centuries is not only very varied but is also heavily dependent on ideas brought in from outside. As in the early days of French and British colonization of the province, the house designs presently imported are less sensitive to the place and its unique characteristics and more sensitive to the mass taste of New England or Middle America.

Those who have attempted to distill Nova Scotian designs to recreate an essentially regional house have sometimes opted for the shingles, sometimes for the form, sometimes for small window panes or sometimes for straggling forms, but seldom is there a new house that looks both new and believably regional. To move from the pure copy of an historical prototype to the clearly defined epitome of the Nova Scotian house is still somewhere in the future. The houses illustrated show a variety of approaches, but none is so clearly Nova Scotian that it could not have been found in New Brunswick or New Hampshire.

The forms are traditional but are often put together in new ways. The smaller elements are supplied with garage doors, which are a clear indication of the recent date.

Despite the clearly historical form, the location of the front door and the smaller windows give it away. The chimney is also rather obviously not in the traditional location.

Main entry doors are provided with screen doors, but here the insulated glazed door has diagonal strapping in the panel and diagonal snap-in glazing bars, which are quite out of character with the rest of the design.

Windows are also easily spotted for what they really are which, in this case, is a modern bottom awning window with snap-in glazing bars in a new Gothic-like house. The shutters would not cover the window even if they were operable.

A sure sign of recent construction or of upgraded insulation is the attic ventilator, which is a recent legal requirement, essential when the roof is well insulated.

When the design displays an attitude towards the historical precedents, yet manages to subtly change all the parts, it becomes a new thing altogether. The steep roof and the board and batten walls are compatible yet make up a new style, not Gothic Revival.

Porter's Lake

Lunenburg

Sherbrooke

Halifax

Lunenburg Co.

1970+

Cedar

As the "split-level" was an inappropriate design solution for a flat site, so too the exposed western red cedar or redwood siding on recent Nova Scotian houses appears equally inappropriate. The transport cost for the 7,000 km journey seems extravagant and questionable. Not all the houses illustrated are of cedar, so the name is generally descriptive rather than specific to one specie of wood.

There is no rigid ruling observed in these designs. Look for the direction of the joints: horizontal, vertical, 45 degree angled or angled to match the pitch of the roof. Within this group, it sometimes seems as if design is generated less from a concern for the shapes and forms of houses and more from a concern over the cost of repainting. The intention that the extra cost of the cedar will be recouped over the life of the building through the elimination of painting appears to be a false assumption.

Even the casual observer will notice that there are few traditional shapes in this group and that many are based on a pulling-apart of the composition of the house, especially the stairs, with glass used in the gaps between the blocks. The forms on which the cladding is applied show influences that range from the European-based International style all the way to the Californian low-pitched ranch and the very influential Sea Ranch housing of the late 1960s. It is curious that the architecture of Sea Ranch is often copied out of sight of water and protected from wind.

A small house, built in the 1970s, used Eastern cedar shingles rather than Western cedar boarding. The architect posed a question that is relevant to the design of all houses. Why import materials and then a style to suit them? It can be seen by the brief time that this style was in vogue that many chose an alternative way. The very modest little cedar-shingled house at Prospect makes a loud comment out of all proportion with its size.

Diagonal boarding marks the entry. The form has been made complex by the subtraction of the face and the cutaway corner. Stain has unified the appearance and partly suppressed the board pattern.

Vertical boarding and a flat roof spell economy, while the simple forms suggest that space has been made the priority. Expression of the floor levels in the cladding is unusual and suggests a European influence.

Fragmented roofs all belonging to the same family through a common roof pitch have been a recent fashion. The extravagance of form and increased heat loss are in direct contrast to the energy crisis.

Horizontal clapboarding is less common than vertical boarding on modern houses. Vertical boarding is here used only on the curved stair tower.

Here, a complex arrangement of geometry is further complicated by the use of the sloping boards. The vertical boarding is used to accent the changes in form but instead helps add to the confusion.

This is an essentially modern interpretation of the Nova Scotian idiom that humbly puts the emphasis into the form and plays down the decorative alternatives. The recessed corners are entirely new, but this house is surely rooted in regional history, in both scale and imagery.

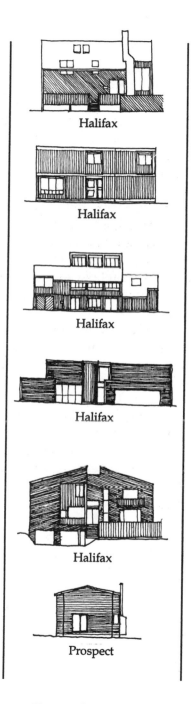

Halifax

Halifax

Halifax

Halifax

Halifax

Prospect

1960+

Mobile

The baby boom that followed World War II resulted in a housing boom twenty years later. For many aspiring homeowners the trailer or mobile home was the only affordable solution. Maintenance costs on a trailer are typically small and, unless it is blown over in a storm, a mobile home can provide a good housing solution. Two types of development have resulted: privately-owned individual sites and trailer parks. The latter have often resulted in crowded conditions and a lack of individuality or identity. Many young people have preferred to put a Mobile on their own land as their first home.

Given time, the trailer may be improved. The first alteration away from Mobile is to provide a permanent foundation, sometimes as usable basement. Next the entrance is modified to enclose the inevitable flight of steps and provide a vestibule and storage space.

When an extension is needed there may be an addition as simple as a lean-to, or if the trailer is doubled in size there may be a new roof as well, so that the original trailer is swallowed up in a house form. In other cases, where no extra accommodation is required, the exterior may undergo considerable change with panelling becoming shingles and curved roof becoming pitched. One visually significant alteration is to see how much difference even a small overhang makes.

Sometimes the roof is left with its metal finish and loaded down with old tires to prevent drumming or wind lift. On exposed sites there may be a requirement for guy ropes to prevent toppling in a high wind.

Nearly six percent of the population of Nova Scotia lives in mobile homes.

The long narrow form of the mobile home is camouflaged in various ways but is shown first in its simplest form—on a fixed site. This one has been enclosed between floor and ground and has had a pitched roof added.

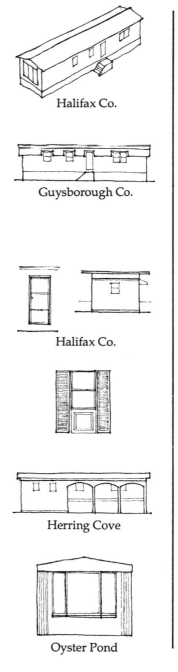

Halifax Co.

The most common way to manipulate the form is through the roof shape and overhang. Unless placed directly onto a prepared foundation, the height of floor above grade cannot easily be reduced, making the entry steps prominent. A mansard roof is used to reduce visible wall height.

Guysborough Co.

Although doors start off being exposed or covered by a screen door, they quickly get enclosed by a porch for greater heat savings and for storage.

Halifax Co.

Windows are plain to patterned, with some having panels beneath and shutters beside them. The intention is to exaggerate the height and so reduce the apparent length of the trailer.

Ultimately a number of Mobiles have been swallowed up by their additions, which accrue slowly. The first stage may be the extended porch, here at extreme scale.

Herring Cove

Decoration is limited to the surface of the shell or to the ends. A bay window may be provided for an end bedroom as easily as for a livingroom.

Oyster Pond

Any age

Vacation

Some of the older houses in out-of-the-way places have been turned into second homes, and in other cases second houses have been built specially for vacationers. The first category have been covered under their individual styles, regardless of current use, but in the latter group are a number of interesting and odd houses, usually not very visible from the highway but sometimes worth seeking out.

One distinction between summer and winter Vacation houses arises from their obviously different requirements for space heating, and the size of the wood pile may give a clue to their use. In the case of the modern purpose-designed Vacation house there may be a reliance on passive solar heating, but often security shutters are more important than heat.

Function will often dictate siting—summer or winter use being related to sea, lake or hillside; however, with crosscountry skiing becoming more popular, siting Vacation houses is really not constrained in the way it used to be.

The style of some cottages or camps is very much dependent on the availability of materials. An odd assortment of sale price windows and doors may be assembled in a second-hand envelope for the do-it-yourself enthusiast who enjoys making things, especially to express individuality. Some Vacation houses are extremely odd!

Some houses are specially designed and may be quite extravagant in their plate glass views of the scenery, with boat ramps and carports as integral bits of the design. There are even a few small palaces, but these are very exclusively isolated, well hidden, except from the water, and often used intermittently all year round.

One room is all that many vacationers require. In its simplest form there may be a porch and a chimney as well.

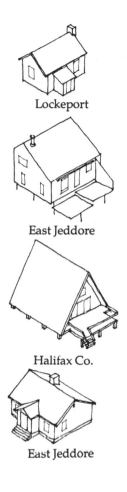

Lockeport

A modern cottage may relate to history through form, to the ground by large decks, to extended use with a wood stove chimney and to economy with post foundations.

East Jeddore

The A-frame form minimizes the wall area and speeds construction as well as reducing costs. It restricts headroom, but to many this is also a way to generate coziness.

Halifax Co.

Adaptive use of small houses to intermittent use has been a large source of vacation houses, often remaining where originally built.

East Jeddore

Few can aspire to real luxury, but for some the vacations are just seasonal excursions to another house. Alexander Graham Bell was one such fortunate man whose Vacation house was winterized.

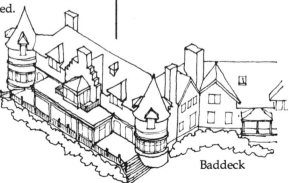

Baddeck

1960+

Rehabilitation
Few houses remain untouched over time; some are altered several times during their lifetime and many are altered beyond all recognition. This classification is mentioned here, as the pressure to change existing houses seems much greater at present than it has been for many years. With rising costs of property, land and buildings, and especially rising energy costs, the need to choose between town or country living, between old or new housing, or the right location but the wrong house, puts us into a new era of building attitudes. Rehabilitation, whether gut and replace, "gentrify," or merely upgrade, makes up the majority of the Canadian building industry.

Reconstruction of a house including exterior finish, windows, doors, insulation and roofing, can be done in two ways. First is the exact replication of everything that was there without any visible sign that anything has happened, at least at a distance. The second method is to assume that the site is more valuable than the house and to change the building to suit modern needs, regardless of the extent of alteration, such as the insertion of a whole new storey.

In many cases the reconstruction is only of a part, as a porch or set of steps needs replacement, and the design changes slowly through incrementally small changes. In other cases storm windows make a drastic visual difference, and in yet others the alteration of a roof slope or dormer window design can totally change the appearance.

Changing tall Victorian vertical sliding sash windows into modern small horizontal sliding windows may be disruptive, altering the scale and balance.

Although the scale of alteration varies considerably, the variation in the attitude of the person behind the change seems even greater in scope. Rehabilitation may vary from gross vandalism all the way to totally faithful restoration.

In order to save money on maintenance and energy, but at the cost of its integrity, this building has been stripped of its decoration, doors and windows for alternatives that are all poorer in quality. The basic form is all that remains, but even here the entry has been moved off-centre.

Unfortunately there are many examples of pairs of houses in which the original harmony has been destroyed by the non-cooperation of neighbours.

The ultimate in false restoration! The vinyl-clad pediment uses siding without mouldings, the insulated door has diamond-shaped snap-in glazing bars, and the mail boxes are at the wrong heights for the mailman.

Removing vertical windows and replacing them with horizontal ones completely changes the scale and proportion of the façade. Strangely enough, the vertical window may function rather better than the horizontal one.

Probably the most dramatic change in appearance is made by the scale of the siding material. Narrow courses of shingles or width of clapboard are often replaced by wider siding, which discloses its true material nature at the longitudinal joints.

Fortunately some good examples do exist where at least on the outside there is harmony.

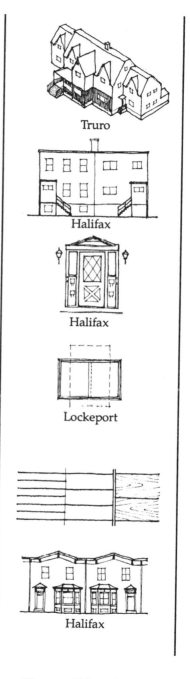

Truro

Halifax

Halifax

Lockeport

Halifax

1980+

Post
Modern

As the last style to be discussed in this book, the Post Modern is perhaps the most likely to sum up the trends of fashion in architecture down through the centuries. As the name implies, Post Modern is "after modern" and is a reaction to the stark simplicity of that style and its simple derivatives. Post Modern harks back to earlier times and, once again, Classical columns, pediments and Palladian windows are used, but not in the traditional ways. In many cases the symmetry is purposely distorted or the windows are obviously square, unlike the proportional rectangular windows used in the eighteenth-century precedents. Colour is used, often vibrant and eyecatching, on the exteriors of buildings. Although the overall tonal values may be pastel, juxtaposition of red, orange and pink can set teeth on edge.

Most noticeable of the new features is an extremely self-assured rejection of the old rules of composition. Symmetry may be suggested, but not followed through. Asymmetry, with twists and bends in the circulation routes and even the walls of spaces, demonstrates intellectual virtuosity on the part of the architect, but the designs can easily remain as essays, understood only by other architects. Unfortunately many of the design rules are broken at the cost of a calm harmony that was apparent in the earlier buildings that these buildings sometimes even actively ridicule.

Post Modern might have a short life expectancy. Styles that have grown to become indigenous, that epitomize place as well as era, are usually more immediately embraced by society as a whole. Post Modern appears elitist at the moment.

If Nova Scotia is renowned for the unreliability of the weather, there is now a parallel in architecture. Who knows what will happen? Post Modern could well be the contemporary vehicle for another spate of extravagant experimentation. It will be interesting to see where it goes.

Forms may be simple in outline, but complex in the pattern of openings. This vertical form, though small in size, is heroic in scale due to the marked symmetry of the façade.

Halifax

From a distance, symmetry, gables, dormers and traditional shapes may hide the newness of the style.

1987 Halifax

Details such as the column to the left of the door may shock because they are radically new. In this case, glass block surrounding a stainless steel column lights up at night.

1982 Halifax Co.

The square and the foursquare window are an obvious shift from the earlier rectangular window proportions.

1986 Halifax Co.

Whole elements, such as this tower, may display the virtuosity of the current thinking. Shapes are reminiscent of history and yet each part tells a new story, as does a story within a story.

1982 Halifax Co.

Houses of Nova Scotia 139

Sources of Information

Photographic Collections

Nova Scotia Museum, including the Arthur W. Wallace Collection.

Public Archives of Nova Scotia, including the collections of: Notman Studio, W.L. Bishop, Siffroi Pothier, Philip Hartling, Bridgetown Album #24, Queen's County Historical Collection, Port Medway Album #2.

Province of Nova Scotia, Department of Culture, Fitness and Recreation, Heritage Unit, including special recording of Sydney, Antigonish County, Annapolis County, and Kings County.

Private Collections of Allen Penney and Teresa Janik.

Bibliography

Architecture in general

Blumenthal, John J. G. *Identifying American Architecture*. W.W. Norton, NY, 1981.

Brunskill, R.W. *Illustrated Handbook of Vernacular Architecture*. Faber & Faber, London, 1978.

Dixon, Rand Multhesius, S. *Victorian Architecture*. Thames and Hudson, London, 1978.

Downing, A.J. *The Architecture of Country Houses*. Dover, New York, 1969.

Dunbar, J.G. *The Architecture of Scotland*. Batsford, London, 1978.

Fleming, J., Honour, H., Pevsner, N. *The Penguin Dictionary of Architecture*. Penguin, Harmondsworth, 1972.

Foley, Mary Mix. *The American House*. Harper and Row, New York, 1981.

Gowans, Alan. *Images of American Living*. Harper and Row, New York, 1976.

Hamlin, Talbot. *Greek Revival Architecture in America*. Dover, New York, 1964.

Handlin, D.P. *The American Home*. Little, Brown, Boston, 1979.

Hitchcock, H.R. *Architecture: Nineteenth and Twentieth Centuries*. Penguin, Harmondsworth, 1978.

Kimball, Fiske. *Domestic Architecture of the American Colonies and of the Early Republic*. Dover, New York, 1966.

Lloyd, Nathaniel. *A history of the English House*. Architectural Press, London, 1976.

Moore, C., Allen, G., Lyndon, D. *The Place of Houses*. Holt Rinehart & Winston, New York, 1979.

Pevsner, Nikolaus. *A History of Building Types*. Princeton, 1976.

Pierson, William H. *American Buildings and their Architects, Colonial & NeoClassical Styles*. Anchor, New York, 1976.

Pierson, William H. *American Buildings and their Architects, Technology & the Picturesque*. Anchor, New York, 1980.

Poppeliers, J., Chambers, S.A., Schwartz, N.B. *What Style is it?* Preservation Press, Washington, 1980.

Rifkind, Carole. *A Field Guide to American Architecture*. New

American Library, New York, 1980.

Scott, H.S. *A Dictionary of Building.* Penguin, Harmondsworth, 1974.

Vaux, Calvert. *Villas and Cottages.* Dover, New York, 1970.

Architecture, Canada

Arthur, E. *Architecture.* Section in Encyclopedia Canadiana, pp 190-197, 1970.

Brosseau, G. *Gothic Revival in Canadian Architecture.* Canadian Historic Sites, Number 25, Ottawa, 1980.

Byers, M., Kennedy, J., McBerney, M. *Rural Roots.* University of Toronto Press, 1977.

Cameron, C., Wright, J. *Second Empire Style in Canadian Architecture.* Canadian Historic Sites, Number 24, Ottawa, 1980.

Canada Mortgage Housing Corporation. *Canadian Housing Design Council. Awards for Residential Design, 1976-1977.* Ottawa, 1978.

Humphreys, B.A., Sykes, M. *The Buildings of Canada.* The Readers Digest Association, Montreal, 1974.

Jackson, A. *The Future of Canadian Architecture.* Tech Press, Halifax, 1979.

Kalman, H. *The Sensible Rehabilitation of Older Houses.* CMHC, Ottawa, 1979.

Lessard, M., Marquis, H. *Encyclopedie de la Maison Quebecoise.* Les Editions de l'Homme, Montreal, 1972.

Moogk, P.N. *Building a House in New France.* McClelland and Stewart, Toronto, 1977.

Rempel, J.I. *Building with Wood.* University of Toronto Press, Toronto, 1980.

Ritchie, T. *Canada Builds.* 1967.

Architecture, Nova Scotia

City of Halifax Planning Department. *An Evaluation & Protection System For Heritage Resources in Halifax.* City of Halifax, Halifax, 1978.

Jensen, L.B. *Country Roads, Rural Pictou County, N.S.* Petheric Press, Halifax, 1974.

Kennickell, M. *Beyond the Estate.* Lancelot Press, Hantsport, 1981.

Kinsman, G. *Colchester County Century Farms*. Nova Scotia Department of Agriculture and Marketing, Truro, N.S., 1979.

Heritage Trust of Nova Scotia. *Founded Upon a Rock*. Halifax, 1971. *Seasoned Timbers Volume 1*. Heritage Trust, 1972. *Seasoned Timbers Volume 2*. Heritage Trust, 1974. *Lakes, Salt Marshes & the Narrow Green Strip*. Heritage Trust, 1979.

Lunenburg Heritage Society. *A Walk Through Old Lunenburg*. Lunenburg, 1979.

MacDonald, K. *Selected Buildings in Mahone Bay, N.S.* MSS Report No. 260, Parks Canada, Ottawa, 1977.

Moore, C. *Fortress of Louisbourg*. College of Cape Breton Press, Sydney, 1981.

Nova Scotia Association of Architects. *Exploring Halifax*. Greey de Pencier, Toronto, 1976.

Pictou Heritage Society. *Wood and Stone*. Petheric Press, Halifax, 1972.

Port Williams Women's Institute. *The Port Remembers*. Kentville, 1976.

Reilly, S. *Selected Buildings in Yarmouth, N.S.* MSS Report No. 262, Parks Canada, Ottawa, 1977.

Silver, B.C., Kirkconnell, W. *Wolfville's Historic Homes*. Lancelot Press, Wolfville, 1967.

Sunderland, T. *Still Standing*. College of Cape Breton Press, Sydney, 1980.

Wallace, A.W. *Early Buildings of Nova Scotia*. Heritage Trust of Nova Scotia and Nova Scotia Museum, Halifax, 1976.

A TIME CHART OF ARCHITECTURAL STYLES

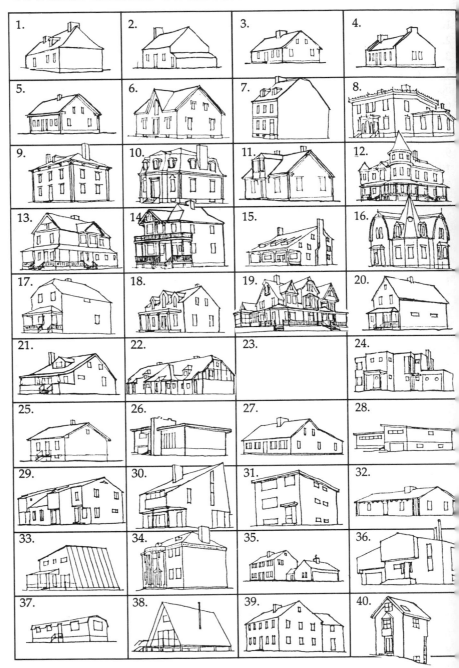

1.
2.
3.
4.
5.
6.
7.
8.
9.
10.
11.
12.
13.
14.
15.
16.
17.
18.
19.
20.
21.
22.
23.
24.
25.
26.
27.
28.
29.
30.
31.
32.
33.
34.
35.
36.
37.
38.
39.
40.